IN ALL HER NAMES

IN ALL HER NAMES

Explorations of the Feminine in Divinity

Edited by
JOSEPH CAMPBELL
and
CHARLES MUSÈS

HarperSanFrancisco
A Division of HarperCollinsPublishers

Library of Congress Cataloging-in-Publication Data

In all her names : explorations of the feminine in divinity / edited by
 Joseph Campbell and Charles Musès.
    p. cm.
  Includes bibliographical references.
  ISBN 0-06-250629-3 (alk. paper)
   1. Femininity of God. 2. Goddesses. I. Campbell, Joseph.
 II. Musès, Charles.
  BL215.5.I5 1991
  291.2' 114—dc20
                           90-55778
                               CIP

91   92   93   94   95   RRD(H)   10 9 8 7 6 5 4 3 2 1

This edition is printed on acid-free paper that meets the American National Standards Institute Z39.28 standard.

CONTENTS

Ayeshah Haleem, Lisa Lyon,
Jacqueline Northfield, and others

Ave Atque Vale

IN ALL HER NAMES

PROLOGUE

Joseph Campbell was not only an esteemed colleague but a dear friend. I vividly remember him, especially some splendid dinner conversations we enjoyed in New York and San Francisco.

After the idea of this book took hold of me in 1984, and the two of us had discussed it at length, Joe felt so strongly about the "Goddess project," as we called it, that he interrupted work on his great *Atlas of World Mythology* to edit the book with me and compose his own substantial contribution (chap. 3), actually the last creative work he was to have time to complete before his passing at the end of October 1987. This is vintage Campbell and he felt that it was, in his own words to me, his "letter to the world."

Although implicit in his writings in many places (for example, the wonderful description of the Lady of the House of Sleep in his popular *Hero with a Thousand Faces* [pp. 110–11] quoted in chap. 4), it is not generally realized that devotion to the perennial Goddess was a deep facet of Joe's own credo. His contribution here bears that out. After his passing, a new friend and colleague, Riane Eisler, entered the scene and graced it, helping to distill the book into a quartet and making a signal contribution of her own (chap. 1), beautifully supplementing that of my long-time colleague Marija Gimbutas (chap. 2) as well as my own researches (chap. 4) into ancient Egyptian and Chinese teachings addressing crucial spiritual-psychological problems today. Finally, an unique epilogue of celebrations closes the book. (The initials *C. M.* in the text refer to the present editor.)

We shall seek to unravel ancient and abiding skeins and explore deep roots and powerful themes of some of the profoundest impulses and inspirations of humanity, and in particular that tap

1

root and blossom affirming Goethe's ultimate vision: *das Ewig-Weibliche zieht uns hinan* (the Eternal Feminine draws us on).

"In All Her Names" is my literal translation of the Ancient Egyptian ritual address (*in ranis nūb:*) to the Great Goddess, mostly known as Isis but also known as "She of a Thousand Names" and "She of the Unlifted Veil at Saïs." As John Cowper Powys, who so deeply influenced D. H. Lawrence, wrote,

> For the great goddess whose forehead is crowned with the Turrets of the Impossible, moves through the generations from one twilight to another; and of her long journeying from revelation to revelation there is no end.

Charles Musès

1

THE GODDESS OF NATURE AND SPIRITUALITY
An Ecomanifesto

RIANE EISLER

In *The Structure of Scientific Revolutions,* scientific historian Thomas Kuhn shows how modern intellectual and social history has been punctuated by scientific paradigm shifts: radical changes in what is considered knowledge or truth. Archeological and religious studies are today in the throes of such a paradigm shift.

While a generation ago archeologists were still talking of Sumer as the "cradle of civilization," we now know that there were many cradles of civilization, all of them thousands of years older than Sumer. As British archeologist James Mellaart writes in *The Neolithic of the Near East,* "urban civilization, long thought to be a Mesopotamian invention, has predecessors at sites like Jericho and Çatal Hüyük, in Palestine and Anatolia, long regarded as backwaters."

Moreover, we now also know that the social organization and belief systems of these early centers of civilization were very different from how we have been taught society always has been—and by implication always will be—structured.

To begin with, these early cradles of civilization seem to have been remarkably peaceful. There is in the archeological record a general absence of fortifications and signs of destruction through armed conquest. In contrast to the motifs we are all so familiar with, there is also a general absence in the art of these societies of images of men killing each other in battle or raping women. Second, these seem to have been remarkably equitable societies where women and the feminine occupied important social positions. In fact, there is overwhelming evidence that while both female and male deities were worshiped in these societies, the highest power in the universe was seen as the feminine power to give and sustain life, the power incarnated in the body of woman.

This new knowledge about a time before divine and temporal power were associated with all-powerful fathers, kings, and lords clearly has important implications for archeologists, students of myth, and religious scholars. But, as was the case with other scientific paradigm shifts, its revolutionary implications are even greater for society at large. It puts at issue the very foundations of a five-thousand-year-old system in which the world was imaged as a pyramid ruled from the top by a male god, with the creatures made in his image (men), in turn divinely or naturally ordained to rule over women, children, and the rest of nature: a system marked by chronic warfare and the equation of "masculinity" with domination and conquest—be it of women, other men, or nature.

Most important, this fundamental paradigm shift in archeological and religious history is directly relevant to our mounting social and ecological crises. For ours is a time when one more war could be our last, a time when both women and men are reexamining conventional assumptions about such basic issues as what is "masculine" and "feminine," and the relationship between the two. It is a time of rapid social change when we are searching for viable alternatives for our future—alternatives that findings from archeological and religious studies now indicate may, in fact, be deeply rooted in millennia-long traditions we are currently reclaiming from our past.

An arresting example is the Gaia hypothesis, a new scientific theory, proposed by biologists James Lovelock and Lynne Margulis, that the Earth is a unified living system designed to give and sustain life. *Gaia* is an ancient Greek name for the Mother Creatrix, one of many names for the female deity worshiped for many thousands of years as the giver and nurturer of life. In the Fertile Crescent she was Nammu, Mother of the Universe; in Egypt she was Nut; in Africa she was called Nana Buluka; in the Americas she was the Goddess of the Serpent Skirt. But while she was invoked by different names in different places, she was everywhere the symbol of our essential unity, of the oneness of all life on this Earth—the Mother from whose womb all life ensues and to whom all life returns at death, like the cycles of vegetation, to be again reborn.

As physicist Fritjof Capra points out, in fundamental ways the Gaia hypothesis marks a break with eighteenth- and nineteenth-century mechanistic, scientific views. But in even more fundamental ways this supposedly radical hypothesis can also be seen as a reconnection with far more ancient traditions. These traditions, we are now learning, were developed over thousands of years in societies where what we today call an ecological consciousness—the evolving awareness that the Earth must be treated with reverence and respect—was a given, just "the way things are."

A NEW LOOK AT OUR PAST—
AND POTENTIAL FUTURE

In the Judeo-Christian Bible, we learn of a male Father Creator, the source of all life. But many of the earliest known creation stories are of a Great Mother: a female giver and nurturer of life, the Goddess of animals, plants, and humans, waters, earth, and sky.

An ancient Sumerian prayer exalts the glorious Nana as "the Mighty Lady, the Creatress." Another old tablet refers to the Goddess Nammu as "the Mother who gave birth to heaven and earth."

In Egypt, the creation of life was attributed to Nut, Hathor, or Isis, about whom it is written, "In the beginning there was Isis, Oldest of the Old. She was the Goddess from whom all becoming Arose."

In Africa, there are legends about Mawu, another name for the Mother Creatrix. And as biblical scholar Raphael Patai writes, in Canaan, Asherah or Ishtar was the "Progenitress of the Gods."

These are all indications that the worship of female deities was integral to our most ancient sacred traditions. And it indeed makes sense that at the dawn of civilization, when we first began to ask the universal questions (Where do we come from before we are born? Where do we go after we die?), we should have observed that most miraculous of all facts: that human life emerges from the body of woman. It would thus have been only logical that our ancestors first imaged our Earth as a Great Mother, a Goddess of Nature and Spirituality who was the divine source of all birth, death, and regeneration.

This logical conclusion is, in fact, verified by the archeological record, by the countless early female figurines that have now been unearthed in sites all over Asia Minor and Europe. Beginning with the Paleolithic, so-called Venus figurines dating back over twenty thousand years ago to the innumerable goddess figures of the Neolithic Age and, even later, of the Bronze Age, these female images evidence millennia-long traditions of worship. Indeed, as Mellaart points out, the recently discovered goddess-centered cultures of Çatal Hüyük and Hacilar clearly establish a religious continuity between what French archeologist André Leroi-Gourhan describes as a female-centered Paleolithic belief system and the great "Mother Goddesses" of archaic and classical times.

But until recently the view that the ancients worshiped primarily gods (that is, male deities) has pervaded both the scholarly and popular literature. Not only has Western society held the belief promulgated by Judeo-Christian religions that God always was (and by implication always will be) male, this male-centered paradigm has also pervaded Western science.

For example, the conventional account of our cultural evolution, spread by popular literature and still taught in most college survey courses, is that it is the story of "man," the hunter-warrior. In accordance with this view, the hundreds of highly stylized, often pregnant, large-hipped carvings of women found in Paleolithic caves were dubbed "Venus figurines"—objects in some ancient, and presumably obscene, "fertility cult." As UCLA archeologist Marija Gimbutas notes, they were even viewed by some scholars as obese, distorted, erotic symbols—in other words, prehistoric counterparts of *Playboy* centerfolds.

But if we really look at these strangely stylized oval figures, it becomes evident that they are representations of the life-giving

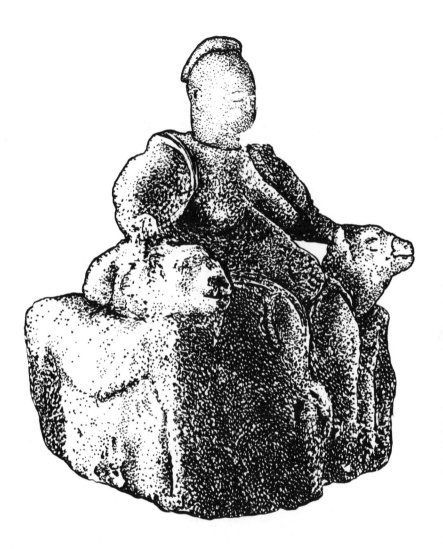

FIG. 1. A goddess figurine found in Çatal Hüyük, Turkey, dating back to 5750 B.C. She is seated on a throne, giving birth, while flanked by what are identified by most authorities as two leopards. What is believed to be the tail of one of the leopards can be seen wrapped over her right shoulder. Line drawing from the original: John Mason.

powers of the world. As Gimbutas, Mellaart, and other archeologists now point out, they are very ancient precursors of the
Great Goddess still revered in historic times as Isis in Egypt, Ishtar
in Canaan, Demeter in Greece, and even later, as the Magna Mater
of Rome and the Catholic Virgin Mary, the Mother of God.

Similarly, earlier scholars kept finding in Paleolithic drawings
and stone and bone engravings what they interpreted as barbed
weapons. But then they could not figure out why in these pictures
the arrowheads or barbs were always going the wrong way. Or
why these "wrong-way weapons" regularly seemed to miss their
mark. Only when these pictures were reexamined by an outsider
to the archeological establishment (not conditioned to see them as
"failed hunting magic") did it become clear that these were not
pictures of weapons. They were images of vegetation: trees and
plants with their branches going exactly the *right* way.

This same view of "man's" nature as a self-centered, greedy,
brutal "born killer" has long shaped what we have been taught
about the next phase of human culture: the Neolithic or agrarian
age. The conventional view, still perpetuated by most college
survey courses, is that the most important human invention—the
development of the technology to domesticate plants—was also
the beginning of male dominance, warfare, and slavery. In this
view, with "man's" invention of agriculture—and thus the possibility of sustaining civilization through a regular, and even sur-
plus, food supply—came not only male dominance but also
warfare and a generally hierarchic social structure.

But once again, the evidence does not bear out the conventional view of civilization as the story of "man's" ever more
efficient domination over both nature and other human beings. To
begin with, anthropologists today generally believe that the
domestication of plants was probably invented by women. Indeed,
one of the most fascinating aspects of the current reclamation of
our lost heritage is the enormous contribution women have made
to civilization. If we closely look at the new data we now have
about the first agrarian or Neolithic societies, we actually see that
all the basic technologies on which civilization is based were
developed in societies that were *not* male-dominant and warlike.

8

FIG. 2. A goddess figurine from Minoan Crete. Done in the highly glazed ceramic technique known as faience, this goddess is one of two similarly bare-breasted "snake goddesses" dating back to the 1600 B.C. Holding snakes in both hands, she also has a cat sitting on top of her head. Felines were a symbol of the Goddess and her priestesses. Hence, after the dominator shift, in keeping with the drive to wholly discredit the earlier ways (the cat was holy in Ancient Egypt), we find the cat now associated with evil and the medieval "witch." Line drawing from the original: John Mason.

Contrary to what we have been taught of the Neolithic or first agrarian civilizations as male-dominant and highly violent, these were generally peaceful societies that traded extensively with their neighbors rather than killing or plundering to acquire wealth. Thanks to far more scientific and extensive archeological excava-

9

tions, we also know that in these highly creative societies women held important social positions as priestesses, craftspeople, and elders of matrilineal clans. Moreover, these were generally equalitarian societies, where, as Mellaart writes, there are no signs of major differences in status based on sex.

This is not to say that these Neolithic societies were ideal utopias. But unlike our societies, they were *not* warlike. They were *not* societies where women were subordinate to men. And they did *not* see our Earth as an object for our exploitation and domination, since in these societies the world was viewed as a Great Mother: a living entity who, in both her temporal and spiritual manifestations, creates and nurtures all forms of life.

This consciousness of the essential unity of all life has in modern times been preserved in a number of tribal cultures, which revere the Earth as our Mother. It is revealing that these cultures have often been described as "primitive" by anthropologists. Equally revealing is that, frequently in these cultures, women traditionally hold key public positions as shamans or wise women and often as heads of matrilineal clans.

This, in turn, leads to an important point that, once articulated, may seem obvious. The way a society structures the most fundamental human relations—the relations between the female and male halves of humanity, without which our species could not survive—has major implications for the *totality* of a social system. It clearly affects the individual roles and life choices of both women and men. Equally important, though until now rarely noted, is that it also profoundly affects all our values and social institutions—whether a society will be peaceful or warlike, generally balanced or authoritarian, and living in harmony with or bent on conquest of our environment.

MYTHICAL CLUES TO A DIFFERENT REALITY

Previously unknown prepatriarchal societies have been coming to light since World War II. Rich evidence has been yielded by the excavation of important sites such as Çatal Hüyük and Hacilar in

Turkey (the largest Neolithic site ever excavated) and what the well-known UCLA archeologist Marija Gimbutas calls the civilizations of Old Europe in the Balkans and Greece (that even had a script thousands of years before Sumer, which Gimbutas and her former student Shawn Winn are attempting to decipher and which scientist Charles Musès has related to phosphenes—primordial images in the brain).*

But just as not so long ago people rejected the scientific finding that the Earth is round not flat, these new scientific findings are today viewed by some people as impossible because they are contrary to everything we have been taught. Yet if we stop and think about it, we have actually had knowledge of this earlier era for a very long time.

Almost all societies have legends about an earlier, more harmonious age. For example, one of the most ancient Chinese legends comes to us from the *Tao Te Ching,* which tells us of a time when the yin, or feminine principle, was not yet subservient to the male principle, or yang, a time when the wisdom of the mother was still honored above all. Hesiod, the Greek poet who wrote about the same time as Homer, also tells of this earlier more peaceful time now being revealed by the archeological spade. He writes of an age when this earth was inhabited by a golden race who "tilled their fields in peaceful ease" (in other words, the Neolithic Age) before a lesser race brought with them Ares, the Greek god of war.

In fact, some of the most fascinating clues to this earlier time come to us from no less a source than the best-known story of Western civilization: the story of the Garden of Eden. What this story tells us is that there was once a garden where man and woman (Adam and Eve) lived in harmony with one another and with nature. Since the invention of agriculture made possible the first gardens on this Earth, the garden in the story could be a reference to the Neolithic Age—when our ancestors planted the first gardens on this Earth.

---

*See Charles Musès, *Destiny and Control in Human Systems* (Boston: Kluwer-Nijhoff, 1985), 109ff.

The fact that Eve would take counsel from a serpent is also explained by the mythical and archeological data. For in earlier times the serpent was a symbol of the Goddess's oracular wisdom—as still evidenced in historical times by the association of the serpent (the python) with the high priestess (the pythoness) who gave divinely inspired counsel to Greek heads of state at the famous oracular shrine at Delphi. Even the question of what brought this earlier era to a close is answered in the biblical story. This lost "paradise" was a time before a male god decreed woman be subservient to man: in other words, a time when society was *not* dominated by men, when women and men lived and worked together in equal partnership.

We have been taught our Fall from paradise is an allegory of God's punishment of man—and particularly of woman—for the sin of disobeying Jehovah's orders not to eat from the tree of knowledge. But what the archeological evidence reveals is that this story [like the Babylonian myths from which it derives] is based on folk memories of a time before [as the Bible also tells us] brother turned against brother and man trod woman down under his heel.

The punishment of Eve for her refusal to acknowledge Jehovah's monopoly of the tree of knowledge is a mythical device to justify male dominance and authoritarian rule. But the underlying story, with critical significance for our time, is that it records a major social shift. This shift, now being extensively verified by the archeological evidence, is the dramatic change that occurred in our prehistory from a far more egalitarian and peaceful way of living on this Earth to the violent imposition of a system of human rankings (beginning with the ranking of the male half of humanity over the female half) based on force or the threat of force.

IF IT ISN'T PATRIARCHY, MUST IT BE MATRIARCHY?

Already in the nineteenth century, when archeology was still in its infancy, scholars found evidence of societies where women were not subordinate to men. But their interpretation of this evidence was that, if these societies were not patriarchies, they must have been matriarchies. In other words, if men did not dominate women, then women must have dominated men.

However, the conclusion that in prepatriarchal societies men were oppressed by women is not borne out by the evidence. Rather, it is a function of what I have called a *dominator* society worldview. The real alternative to patriarchy is not matriarchy, which is only the other side of the dominator coin. The alternative, now revealed to be the original direction of our cultural evolution, is a *partnership* society: a way of organizing human relations in which—beginning with the most fundamental difference in our species, the difference between female and male—diversity is *not* equated with inferiority or superiority.

What we have until now been taught as history is only the history of dominator societies: the record of the male-dominant, authoritarian, and highly violent civilizations that began approximately five thousand years ago. For example, the conventional view is that the beginning of European civilization is marked by the emergence in ancient Greece of the Indo-Europeans. But the new archeological evidence demonstrates that the arrival of the so-called Indo-Europeans actually marks the truncation of European civilization.

As Gimbutas extensively documents, there was in Greece and the Balkans an earlier civilization, which she calls the civilization of Old Europe. The first Indo-European invasions [by pastoralists from the arid steppes of the northeast she calls the Kurgans] foreshadow the end of a matrifocal, matrilineal, peaceful agrarian era. Like fingerprints in the archeological record, we see evidence of wave after wave of barbarian invaders from the barren fringes of the globe. It is they who bring with them their angry gods of thunder and war and who everywhere leave destruction and devastation in their wake.

At this point, the archeological landscape shows dramatic evidence of a radical social and cultural shift. We see the disappearance of millenial traditions of art and pottery and a sharp decrease in the size of settlements. There is also the appearance of "suttee" chieftain tombs [so called because with the robust male skeleton are sacrificed women, children, and animals to serve him even after death]. Warfare and male dominance now also become endemic, as a communally based system is replaced by "strongman" rule.

Along with these signs of radical changes in social structure, we also see signs of a radical shift in belief system and values. One of the most striking manifestations of this change is found in the art, which reflects a dramatic transformation of myth, since these invaders, as Gimbutas writes, literally "worshipped the power of the lethal blade." Strongman rule becomes idealized, even presented as divinely ordained, in an art that glorifies killing [scenes of "heroic" battles] and rapes [as in Zeus's fabled rapes of both mortal women and goddesses].

And so gradually, in the service of their earthly and divine lords and kings, the artists, bards, scribes, and priests of the ruling men replace the matrifocal, female-oriented myths and images of the civilization of Old Europe. But so strong is the memory of an earlier and better time that, albeit in distorted form, it still lingers on. But now it is only found in folk stories and legends about what is increasingly presented as only an imaginary past.

THE LOST ATLANTIS?

In the nineteenth century, the archeological excavations of Sophia and Heinrich Schliemann established that the Homeric story of the Greek sacking of Troy, long considered only an imaginary fable, was historically based. Similarly, the probable historical basis for the legend of Atlantis is now being revealed by twentieth century archeological excavations.

The fabled civilization of Atlantis was said to have ended when large land masses sank into the sea. What geologists and archeologists now reveal is that approximately thirty-five hundred years ago, due to massive earthquakes and immense tidal waves, the Mediterranean Sea, in fact, swallowed up large masses of land. For example, as in the legend of Atlantis, most of the island of Thera or Santorini at that time sank into the sea.

These cataclysmic events seem to have marked the end of what scholars call Minoan civilization, a highly technologically

14

developed Bronze Age civilization centered in the Mediterranean island of Crete. Minoan Crete had the first paved roads in Europe, even indoor plumbing. In sharp contrast to the much more publicized slave societies of antiquity, Crete had a generally high standard of living. Its houses were built for both beauty and comfort. And its art is so natural, so free, so full of the celebration of life in all its forms that scholars have described it as unique in the annals of civilization.

But what really makes Minoan Crete unique is not only the grace and exuberant joy in life of its art; it is that its social structure and belief system were so very different from that of other "high" civilizations of antiquity. Archeologist Nicolas Platon, the former head of the Acropolis Museum who excavated Crete for over fifty years, notes that this was a society where descent was still traced through the mother and where the influence of women is visible in every sphere. For example, the only Minoan fresco of tribute is not the conventional picture of the aggrandized king with a sword in his hand and kneeling figures at his feet characteristic of ancient male-dominant civilizations. It is rather the picture of a woman. And instead of sitting on an elevated throne, she is standing with her arms raised in a gesture of benediction as men approach her with offerings of fruits, wine, and grains. As Platon also writes, Minoan Crete was a "remarkably peaceful" society. Most strikingly, here "the whole of life was inspired by an ardent faith in the goddess Nature, the source of all creation and harmony." As Platon notes, "this led to a love of peace, a horror of tyranny and a respect for the law."

In other words, Minoan Crete was not a *dominator* society, where power was conceptualized as the capacity to dominate and destroy, symbolized by the blade. In this highly creative and peaceful society, masculinity was *not* equated with domination and conquest. Accordingly, women and the "soft" or "feminine" values of caring, compassion, and nonviolence—which are so despised in stereotypical "masculine" dominator ideology—did not have to be devalued. Power was seen as actualizing power, as the capacity to create and nurture life. It was power to, rather than

FIG. 3. In many cultures the Goddess embodies both nature and spirituality. This is beautifully illustrated in this painting (the original is in vivid color) of the Tecate Native American Grandmother Eagle. As the artist, Timothy Hinchliff, writes: "In Original Times our Grandmother Eagle dreamed that there would be a sacred mountain awakening and she wanted to bring it into being. From her center she sent seeds that grew into boulders that mirrored the shapes of the People, Animals, and Plants to come."

16

© Mayumi Oda

FIG. 4. Today, artists from all over the world are again, as in our prehistory, creating beautiful and evocative images of the Goddess. Some of them, like Mayumi Oda's Japanese Goddess Kwannon, the Japanese form of the Chinese Goddess Kuan Yin (= the Tibetan Chenrezi and the Hindu Buddhist Avalokitésvara *Ed.*), are once again whimsical as well as colorful. Mayumi Oda writes of this image: "The Goddess is coming to you. Can you come to her?"

17

power over: the power to illuminate and transform human consciousness [and with it reality] that is still in our time symbolized by the "feminine vessel," the Chalice or Holy Grail.

NATURE AND SPIRITUALITY

In our epics and much of our classical and popular literature, we have been taught that "real" men may not be too "soft" or "feminine." We have also been taught that religion is the spiritual realm and, just as men are superior to women, spirituality is superior to nature. But for our goddess-worshiping ancestors, there were no such sharp polarities between "masculine" and "feminine" and "spirituality" and "nature."

In sharp contrast to patriarchal religions [where only men can be priests, rabbis, bishops, lamas, Zen masters, and popes], we know from Minoan, Egyptian, Sumerian, and other ancient records that women were priestesses. Indeed, the highest religious office appears to have been that of high priestess in service of the Goddess. And the Goddess herself was not only the source of all life and nature; she was also the font of spirituality, mercy, wisdom, and justice.

As the Sumerian Goddess Nanshe, she sought "justice for the poor and shelter for the weak." The Egyptian Maat was also the Goddess of Justice. The Greek Goddess Demeter was known as the lawgiver, the bringer of civilization, dispensing mercy and justice. As the Celtic Cerridwen, she was the Goddess of Intelligence and Knowledge. And it is Gaia, the Primeval Prophetess of the shrine of Delphi, who in Greek mythology is said to have given the golden apple tree [the tree of knowledge] to her daughter, the Goddess Hera. Moreover, the Greek Fates, the enforcers of laws, are female. And so also are the Greek Muses, who inspire all creative endeavor.

Even in the Bible, where the only mention of the Goddess is as the Queen of Heaven whom patriarchal prophets such as Jeremiah rail against, we see that in ancient times the deity was seen as the embodiment of the heavenly or spiritual as well as the earthly or natural. In fact, this association of woman with the highest spirituality—with both wisdom and mercy—survived well into historical times. Even though women were by then already barred from positions of spiritual power, Sophia [the Greek word for wisdom] is still female. So also is the French *sagesse*, the Italian *sapienza*, and the Hebrew word for wisdom, *hochmah*. And even though we have not been taught to think of her this way, the Catholic Virgin Mary [now the only mortal figure in the Christian holy family of divine father and son] still perpetuates the image of the Goddess as the Merciful Mother.

We also know from a number of contemporary tribal societies that the separation between nature and spirituality is not universal. The way tribal people think of nature is generally in spiritual terms. They speak of spirits of nature that must be respected, indeed revered. And we also know that, in many of these tribal societies, women as well as men can be shamans or spiritual healers and that descent in these tribes is frequently traced through the mother.

In sum, *both* nature and woman can partake of spirituality in societies that orient to a partnership model. Jacob Boehme, early in the seventeenth century, saw this clearly as Musès's study of him noted. There is here no need for a false dichotomy between a "masculine" spirituality and a "feminine" nature. The reason is that there is here no need to proclaim the superiority of one over the other, of spirit over nature, of man over woman. Moreover, since in ancient partnership societies woman and the Goddess were identified with *both* nature and spirituality, neither woman nor nature were devalued and exploited.

TOWARD A NEW SPIRITUALITY:
A MANIFESTO FOR MOTHER EARTH

The new knowledge of our past now being reclaimed signals a way out of our alienation from one another and from nature. For even what frequently passes for "higher" spirituality in a dominator society is stunted and distorted, as what this system requires is that spirituality be equated with a detachment that often condones and encourages indifference to avoidable human suffering—as in many Eastern religions. Or it leads to the Western dualism that often in the name of spirituality justifies the domination of culture over nature, of man over woman, of technology over life, and of high priests and other so-called spiritual leaders over "common" women and men.

There is today much talk of a new spirituality, of an evolving high consciousness, not only as a passport to a better life after death, but as a prerequisite for sustaining and enhancing life on this Earth. Our reconnection with millennia-long traditions of respect and reverence for our Mother Earth—traditions in which neither nature nor woman were seen as objects for men's exploitation and domination—may be a key component in this more evolved consciousness.

For ours is a time when the lethal power of the blade has been multiplied a millionfold by nuclear bombs. It is a time when even our rivers, our oceans, and the air we breathe warn us that our ecosystem, our Great Mother Earth, will no longer tolerate a species that has so vilely turned against itself and all life; a time of unprecedented social and technological change when a fundamental paradigm shift is not only possible but necessary if we are to avoid a nuclear and/or ecological holocaust.

Poised on the brink of ecocatastrophe, we gain the courage to look at the world anew, to reverse custom, to transcend our limitations, to break free from the conventional constraints, the conventional views of what is knowledge and truth.

If we look only at part of a picture, we see only part of its story. And if we tell only part of a story, we conceal and distort the truth. If instead we look at the whole picture—at humanity's emergence on this beautiful planet, at our species synergistic partnership with nature, at the whole span of human culture, technology, and spirituality—we not only gain a new view of our past, we also see new possibilities for our future.

We see how the human thirst for creation rather than destruction, so long distorted and suppressed, is once again on the ascendancy, as women and men all over the world are reclaiming our most ancient consciousness—the consciousness of our oneness with one another and our Mother Earth. We see how the leading edge social movements of our time—the peace, feminist, and ecology movements, and all the modern movements for social and economic justice—are deeply rooted in very ancient traditions. And we also see that the more peaceful and just society we are now trying to construct is not an impossible dream but a realistic possibility rooted in the original direction of our cultural evolution.

While there is still time, let us fulfill our promise. Let us fulfill our responsibility to ourselves and to our Great Mother, this wondrous planet Earth. For ourselves and for the sake of our children and their children, let us put aside what we have mislearned during the terrible centuries when we were ruled by the blade. Let us teach our sons and daughters that men's conquest of nature, of women, and of other men is not a heroic virtue; that we have the knowledge and the capacity to survive; that we need not blindly follow our previous bloodstained path to planetary death.

Let us reaffirm our ancient covenant, our sacred bond with our Mother Earth, Goddess of Nature and Spirituality. Let us once again honor the "feminine" power to create and enhance life—and let us understand that this power is not woman's alone but also man's.

All that we so yearn for—the lost sense of wonder, the feeling of connection, the joyful enchantment at the beauty and the mystery of life on our Earth—all these are ours to regain. Let us give back to our hearts and minds the power that is ours and allow our cultural evolution to resume its interrupted course. Let us reconnect with our deepest spiritual roots, so we may use modern technology not to destroy, exploit, and oppress but to free our unique human capacities to love and to create and to again live in partnership, rather than domination, with our miraculous planet, our Mother Earth.

References

Bachofen, J. J. *Myth, Religion, and Mother Right*. Princeton, N.J.: Princeton University Press, 1967.

Blakney, R. B., ed. *The Way of Life: Tao Te Ching*. New York: Mentor, 1955.

Divale, William, and Marvin Harris. "Warfare and the Male Supremacist Complex." *American Anthropologist* 78 (1976): 521–38.

Eisler, Riane. *The Chalice and the Blade: Our History, Our Future*. San Francisco: Harper & Row, 1987.

Eisler, Riane, and David Loye. "Peace and Feminist Theory: New Development." In *World Encyclopedia of Peace*. London: Pergamon Press, 1986.

Eliade, Mircea. *Myth and Reality*. New York: Harper Torchbooks, 1963.

Gimbutas, Marija. "The First Wave of Eurasian Steppe Pastoralists into Copper Age Europe." *The Journal of Indo-European Studies* 5, no. 4 (Winter 1977): 277–338.

––––––. *The Goddesses and Gods of Old Europe, 6500–3500 B.C.* Berkeley: University of California Press, 1982.

Graves, Robert, and Raphael Patai. *Hebrew Myths: The Book of Genesis*. New York: McGraw-Hill, 1963.

Harrison, Jane. *Prolegomena to the Study of Greek Religion*. 1903. Reprint. London: Merlin Press, 1962.

Hawkes, Jacquetta. *Dawn of the Gods: Minoan and Mycenaean Origins of Greece*. New York: Random House, 1968.

Hawkes, Jacquetta, and Sir Leonard Woolley. *Prehistory and the Beginning of Civilization*. New York: Random House, 1963.

Henderson, Hazel. "The Warp and the Weft—The Coming Synthesis of Eco-philosophy and Eco-feminism." *Development*, no. 4 (1984).

Hesiod. "Works and Days." In *An Introduction to Early Greek Philosophy*, edited by John Mansley Robinson. Boston: Houghton Mifflin, 1968.

James, E. O. *The Cult of the Mother Goddess*. London: Thames and Hudson, 1959.

Leroi-Gourhan, Andre. *Prehistoire de l'Art Occidental*. Paris: Edition D'Art Lucien Mazenod, 1971.

Levy, G. Rachel. *Religious Conceptions of the Stone Age and Their Influence upon European Thought*. New York: Harper Torchbooks, 1963.

Lovelock, James. *Gaia*. New York: Oxford University Press, 1979.

Luce, J. V. *The End of Atlantis*. London: Thames and Hudson, 1968.

McConahay, Shirley, and John McConahay. "Sexual Permissiveness, Sex-Role Rigidity, and Violence Across Cultures," *Journal of Social Issues* 33, no. 1 (1977): 134–43.

Marinatos, Spyridon. "The Volcanic Destruction of Minoan Crete." *Antiquity* 13 (1939): 425–39.

Marshack, Alexander. *The Roots of Civilization*. New York: McGraw-Hill, 1972.

Mellaart, James. *Çatal Hüyük*. New York: McGraw-Hill, 1967.

————. *The Neolithic of the Near East*. New York: Charles Scribner's Sons, 1975.

Musès, Charles. *Illumination on Jacob Boehme*. New York: Columbia University Press, 1951 (2d enlarged edition forthcoming).

————. *Destiny and Control in Human Systems*. Boston: Kluwer-Nijhoff, 1985.

Patai, Raphael. *The Hebrew Goddess*. New York: Avon, 1978.

Pietial, Hilkka. "Women As An Alternative Culture: Here and Now." *Development*, no. 4 (1984).

Platon, Nicolas. *Crete*. Archeologia Mundi Series. Geneva: Nagel Publishers, 1966.

Rockwell, Joan. *Fact in Fiction: The Use of Literature in the Systematic Study of Society*. London: Routledge and Kegan Paul, 1974.

Ruether, Rosemary R. *Sexism and God-Talk: Toward a Feminist Theology*. Boston: Beacon Press, 1983.

Spretnak, Charlene. *Lost Goddesses of Early Greece*. Boston: Beacon Press, 1981.

Stone, Merlin. *When God Was a Woman*. New York: Harvest, 1976.

Walker, Barbara G. *The Woman's Encyclopedia of Myths and Secrets*. San Francisco: Harper & Row, 1983.

2

THE "MONSTROUS VENUS"
OF PREHISTORY
Divine Creatrix

MARIJA GIMBUTAS

The term "Palaeolithic Venus" by which the small ancient figurines were first characterized by scholars is obviously an ironic
misnomer. "Venus," commonly understood as the apotheosis of
erotic beauty, as personified by the Indo-European Goddess of
Dawn and Love, is a concept which by no means fits the prehistoric portrayals of women. Palaeolithic as well as subsequent
engravings, reliefs, and sculptures frequently represent the female
body in forms which seem to us absurdly abstract or absurdly
grotesque—so deformed or unrealistically exaggerated as to have
been termed "monstrous" by some prehistorians and art histo-
rians. Only in the recognition of the presence of a preeminent deity
is the class term "Venus" justified.

To this day the prehistoric "Venus" remains a puzzle. Why is
she monstrous? Why "steatopygeous" (with pronounced buttocks)
and with enormous breasts hanging over the equally enormous
belly? Why has she in many portrayals no human head, but only a
snake neck? Why bird-like posteriors? Why was she schematized to
such a degree that only buttocks are modeled, head and legs left as
mere cones? We shall seek some answers to these and other questions and give some hint as to what she may have been.

Over the last hundred years or so, some one thousand engravings, reliefs, and sculptures of female images from the Palaeolithic
period have been found, dating from ca. 33,000 to ca. 9,000 B.C.
The earliest are Aurignacian engravings of vulvas, and the earliest

"Venuses" are from the East Gravettian period of central Europe, dated 27,000–26,000 B.C. Female images are found in a territory of roughly 3000 km. across, between the Pyranees in the west and Siberia in the east. In Europe, most have been found in France, Germany, Czechoslovakia, Italy, and the Ukraine.

Modeling or engraving of the female body or of its parts, such as vulva, breasts, and buttocks, did not stop at the end of the Palaeolithic but continued into the Neolithic and beyond and still survives in corrupted form in graffiti. Clay or marble figurines abound in southeastern and east central Europe of 6500–3500 B.C., their number approaching thirty thousand. Menhirs with female features, figurines, and anthropomorphic pendants or plaques are also known from the central and western Mediterranean and from Atlantic Europe, where they date between ca. 5000 and ca. 2000 B.C. The island of Malta is famous for over life-size goddesses found in temples carved in soft stone as well as miniature figurines of clay and stone. In most of continental Europe, figurine art tapered off during and after 4500–2500 B.C., the period of gradual transformation from female-oriented to male-oriented family and religion. Only in the Aegean and Mediterranean islands and coastal regions did the old tradition persist through the third, and even into the second, millennium B.C.

A number of books and articles published during the present century are dedicated to the problem of "Venuses," and various explanations of why they were made have been offered. Among the more influential are those by Piette (1907), Luquet (1934), Passemard (1938), Hančar (1940), Sacassyn della Santa (1947), Pales (1968), and Delporte (1979), not to mention the general books on prehistoric art where the female images are also cursorily mentioned. The naturalistic forms of painted or carved animals, as more spectacular, have attracted far more attention.

Without going into a detailed review of the various explanations offered, one striking fact should be noted: none of the above mentioned researchers advanced the hypothesis that the images are symbolic or mythical figures, which may have been used to commemorate or reenact seasonal or other rites. The majority of scholars have, however, implied that the "Venuses" have to do with magic or, more concretely, were imbued with the magical power of fecundity. Della Santa, in summarizing the views preceding her (1947), summarized the postulated explanations as follows: the "Venuses" are (1) portraits of real women; (2) aesthetic or erotic ideals; (3) images of fecundity; (4) priestesses; (5) ancestresses. Even in 1979, Delporte, whose book *The Image of Woman in Prehistory* (in French) gives a comprehensive treatment of much that has been written on the subject, adds only the possibility that the "Venuses" may express a symbolic vision of femininity and may therefore portray both mothers and lovers. Leroi-Gourhan, in the luxurious and significant book *The Treasures of Prehistoric Art* (1967), considered it to be premature to speak of the existence of a religious system (although he has shown that the depictions in caves are not random) but emphasized that the system may have been based on opposition and complementarity of male and female values, expressed symbolically by animal figures and by abstract signs.

A new approach was presented by Marshack in *The Roots of Civilization: The Cognitive Beginnings of Man's First Art, Symbol and Notation* (1972). He finds scenes engraved on mobiliary art connected with time-factored ideas, such as the coming of spring, death, and the renewal of life. He sees "storied images" and does not agree with Leroi-Gourhan's polarity of the female and male principles. In my book, *The Gods and Goddesses of Old Europe, 7000–3500 B.C.: Myths, Legends, and Cult Images* (1974), which deals with the figurines and cult objects of Old Europe, I have presented my own conviction that the images—animal, male, or female—are inseparable from the mythical world and that the "Venuses" are either representations of various aspects of the Goddess Creatrix or are portrayals of participants in rituals dedicated to her various aspects and reenacted with the medium of figurine.

In order to approach an understanding of the mythic-cosmogonic system which must have existed in the Upper Palaeolithic, the consideration of later prehistoric materials, such as the treasures of the Neolithic, Chalcolithic, and Copper Age periods of Old Europe (pre-Indo-European Europe) is of utmost importance. It is also necessary to extend research in the direction of the mythological evidence of historic European and Siberian peoples.

The quantities of Neolithic–Copper Age figurines, their association with other cultic objects, their finding in house-shrines or in communal temples on altars or in other well-documented contexts add to the possibility of interpretation or at least to an attempt at relevant meaning. Finding conditions and associations of Palaeolithic female images are rarely known; in most cases the figurines have little or unknown context. With engravings, the situation is better; sometimes a series of female images are engraved in rows or groupings (about five hundred engravings were found at Gönnersdorf, in the Rhine area north of Koblenz: Bosinski, 1968).

The continuity from the Palaeolithic into the Neolithic of the portrayal of certain features of the human female body, which we may call stereotypes, is certain: it is a potent argument for the continuity of a philosophical idea; the repetitious occurrence of certain postures and other peculiarities throughout the millennia cannot otherwise be explained or understood.

The millennial continuity of myth will be here regarded as a principal source in the search for the meaning of the prehistoric "Venuses." I see a single line of development of a religious system from the Upper Palaeolithic through the Neolithic, Chalcolithic, and Copper Age, based on a matrifocal social organization. Old Europe ended, and her cultural system ceased to develop at the beginning of the Indo-European era when a very different social and religious system, dominated by males and male gods, began to supersede it. Thus the era of female dominance in religion is documented as continuous throughout some twenty-five thousand years.

After the major part of Europe was Indo-Europeanized in the period between 4500 and 2500 B.C., the two cultural systems were more or less fused, the Old European system continuing as an undercurrent. The fusion of the two systems can be traced in practically all European mythologies. Even present myths, composed of many layers and with an accretion of features acquired

28

through time, often retain the ancient features of certain figures at the core of the myth. This is particularly true in the myths of cosmogony, where the most ancient aspects of the Goddess Creatrix appear. In many beliefs, fairy tales, riddles, etc. of European peoples, mythical female images continue some characteristics of that prehistoric Goddess of Life, Death, and Regeneration. Even when severely demonized during the Christian era, their archaic features can be reconstructed. Such are the Slavic Baba Jaga and Paraskeva-Pjatnitsa; the Baltic Laima and Ragana; the Irish Machas, Morrigan, or Queen Medb; the Germanic Nerthus; and many others. The Fates—Norns, Moirai, Parcae—the apportioners, givers, and takers, clearly go back to the prehistoric "Venus" and are not Indo-European in origin.

To return to the peculiarities of the Palaeolithic "Venus"—the large vulva, pregnant belly, steatopygy, exaggerated breasts, and schematization of the rest of the body. These peculiarities have a very long life; they occur in the Palaeolithic and Neolithic and cannot, therefore, be accidental occurrences. Consistently, the head, except perhaps for the coiffure, is unimportant. If shown, it rarely has normal human features; sometimes it has a nose or beak, and eyebrows, or is masked. Hands and arms, if present, are reduced, and feet are important only as pegs or stands. The study of the various postures of female images, their association with certain symbolic signs, and their association with cult places in the Neolithic and later, permits the conclusion that there was a long-lasting series of stereotypes or aspects of the Goddess which can be linked with certain philosophical ideas.

We shall first discuss several aspects of the Goddess which link her with the ideas of (1) birth-giving, life-promotion, and regeneration, and (2) life-giving and life-taking, or death.

We begin, therefore, with the period which provides such rich evidence—the Neolithic Copper Age of Old Europe—and project backward. We can also project forward from that time and link various aspects of prehistoric female images with those known from earliest historic periods and the still extant archaic features of European mythologies.

BIRTH-GIVING AND PROMOTION OF LIFE

Among the earliest representations of the human female principle are engravings and reliefs of vulvas from the Aurignacian period (fig. 1). They are conceptually metaphoric, "figural synecdoche" where a part stands for the whole. To show the magic vulva (of the Goddess) was the single purpose of the artist; it was not his object to create a female body but to make corporate a symbol. Such symbolic representation in prehistoric art continued beyond the Palaeolithic. Throughout the Neolithic, Chalcolithic, Copper Age, and even Bronze Age of southern Europe, the concept of the supernatural vulva is expressed as clay triangles or as round pendants with a lens or seed in the center, probably worn as amulets; the symbolic significance of the vulva remained universal throughout Europe for some thirty thousand years!

The key to this symbolism can be seen in associations of the vulva sign with plants and seeds; it is symbolic not of human birth alone but of all birth in nature: plant sprouting, seed germination, springtime, regeneration. Furthermore, the conjunction of the vulva and phallus or, in a different expression, of a more naturalistically portrayed female body with a phallus-shaped neck—a peculiar form that appears both in the Palaeolithic and Neolithic—was apparently the accepted form of depicting life-promotion or the strengthening of life powers (figs. 2–4). This symbolism emerges as philosophical rather than sexual or pornographic.

Further associations are with geometric signs—meanders, chevrons, parallel lines, and nets, symbolic of the aqueous sphere. Good examples of such association are ivory figures from Mezin, in the Ukraine, from the late Upper Palaeolithic, probably 14,000–12,000 B.C. The vulva, engraved over the whole front of the figurine, is the center of attention. Meanders, chevrons, and parallel lines are engraved on the back and sides. The phallic neck and protruding posteriors of some figurines clearly depict a form not quite human but a hybrid of water bird and human female. Here we have an accumulation of symbols linked with the idea of the origin of life: the water sphere, where all life begins, and the magic vulva of the Goddess in combination with her water-bird shape (fig. 5).

Other portrayals of a supernatural vulva appear in figurines in a birth-giving posture or with clearly pregnant bellies and "pregnant" buttocks. These associations, again, have a very long life throughout the Palaeolithic and Neolithic. One example from the Upper Palaeolithic is a miniature figurine of limonite from Monpazier, the Dordogne, southern France (fig. 6). Note the accentuated parts of the body: the large vulva in relief, the pregnant belly, the protruding posterior. There are no arms, and the head is featureless. It is a true "monstrosity" in terms of modern aesthetic norms, but it certainly conveys its symbolic message. As in the Mazin figurines, a combination of symbols links generation and reproduction: the vulva, the pregnant belly, and the protruding posterior, which can be called "pregnant" since always paralleled with the pregnant belly.

The signs incised or painted over such buttocks during the Chalcolithic and Copper Age of Old Europe, as in the illustrations below, characteristically mark such posteriors as symbolic of generation/reproduction. The same combination of exaggerated vulva, belly, and buttocks continues into the agricultural era, even into the Copper Age (fig. 7), asserting the continuity of the popular concept of an image of the Goddess who creates out of her body.

Another closely related symbolic series is figurines in a birth-giving posture, with upraised legs and exposed vulva (fig. 8). The toad/frog-shaped amulets of clay, alabaster, green, or black stone are known from the Neolithic and later times in Europe and must be related to the figurines in the naturalistic birth-giving posture (fig. 9). Several Upper Palaeolithic sculptured and engraved figures with upraised legs may also portray a birth-giving posture. The figurines from Sireuil and Tursac, Dordogne, can be considered as such (fig. 10). The peg of the Tursac figurine may be just a peg— but it may also symbolize the emergence of life or the promotion of life (if it is a phallus). The two lines incised on the peg are probably not accidental; on Old European cult objects the two-line

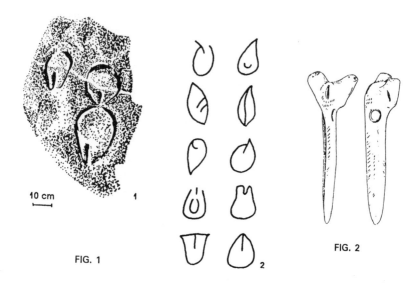

FIG. 1

FIG. 2

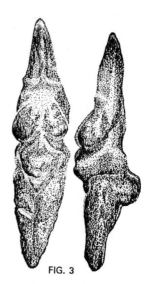

FIG. 1. *1.* Engravings of vulvas on stone slabs from the cave of Blanchard des Roches near Saint-Léon-sur-Vézère, Dordogne, southern France, probably Aurignacian. *2.* vulva or seed signs—engravings from various Palaeolithic sites in southern France.

FIG. 2. A carved schematic figurine of reindeer antler with a raised vulva in the focal position and a long phallic neck marked with chevrons from the cave of Le Placard, Charente, France, of the Magdalenian I–II period. H. 15.3 cm.

FIG. 3. "Venus" with a phallic head, pronounced buttocks, breasts, and a pregnant belly, carved of steatite; Savignano, on the border between the provinces of Bolognia and Modena, Italy. Assumed to be Gravettian (Grimaldian). H. 22.5 cm.

FIG. 3

32

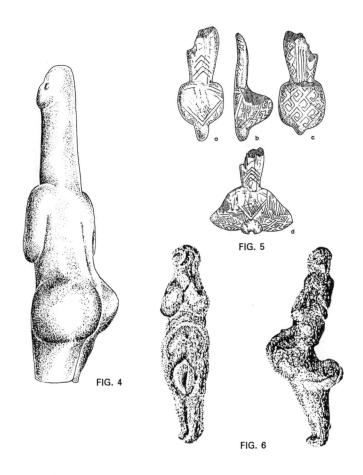

FIG. 4

a   b   c

FIG. 5

d

FIG. 6

FIG. 4. "Steatopygeous" marble figurine with phallic neck from Attica, Greece. Neolithic, problably ca. 6000 B.C.

FIG. 5. Ivory figurine from Mezin, western Ukraine, probably 14,000–12,000 B.C. Note that the shape of the statuette is that of a water-bird shape but has a large human vulva. The figurine is marked with chevrons in front of the neck, and parallel lines and meanders over the back. H. 5 cm.

FIG. 6. Miniature figurine of limonite from Monpazier, Dordogne, southern France, with supernatural vulva, buttocks, and pregnant belly. H. 5.5 cm.

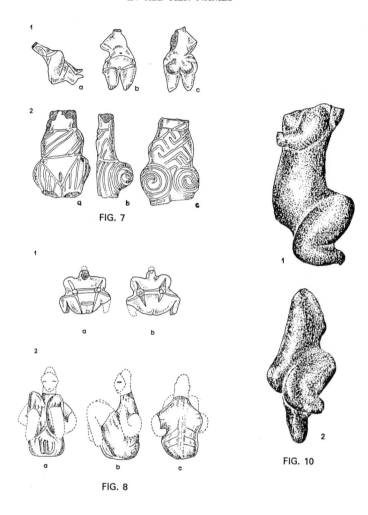

FIG. 7

FIG. 8

FIG. 10

FIG. 7. Neolithic and Chalcolithic terra-cotta figurines with large vulvas and exaggerated buttocks. *1,* Achilleion, Thessaly, classical Sesklo culture, 6100–6000 B.C. *2,* Kalojanovets, central Bulgaria, Karanovo IV, 5200–5100 B.C.

FIG. 8. Figurines in birth-giving posture, *1,* black stone pendant from Achilleion, Thessaly, Ib period, 6400–6300 B.C., proto-Sesklo culture. H. ca. 4 cm. *2,* Terra-cotta figurine (reconstructed) with an exposed vulva, Achilleion, Thessaly, period II, 6300–6200 B.C.

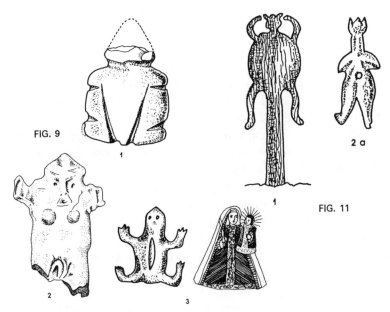

FIG. 9

1

2 a

1

FIG. 11

2

3

FIG. 9. Female-toad hybrids with accentuated vulva, probably epiphanies of the Goddess in the birth-giving aspect. *1*, Neolithic alabaster figurine from Anza, central Macedonia, 5800–5600 B.C. H. ca. 7 cm.; *2*, Maissau, a late Bronze Age cemetery in lower Austria, ca. 1000 B.C.; *3*, from an ex-voto painting in southern Germany, dated A.D. 1811. For 2 and 3, see A. Gulder's "Die urnenfelderzeitliche 'Frauenkröte' von Maissau in Niederösterreich und ihr geistesgeschichtlicher Hintergrund," in *Mitt. d. Prähist. Kommission der Osterreichen Akademie d. Wissenschaften*, 10 (1960): 1–157. [*Editor's note:* In 3, the cleft on the toad's *back* is not a vulva but a symbol of caring, nurture, and protection. In certain viviparous toads, the female has a cleft in her back wherein her tiny offspring stay, as in a quasi-marsupial pouch, venturing forth more and more as they grow older. *C.M.*]

FIG. 10. (*Opposite*) Upper Palaeolithic female images from Dordogne, France, very probably portraying a birth-giving posture. *1*, Sireuil. Calcite. H. 9 cm. (head broken). Considered either Aurignacian or upper Périgordian; *2*, Tursac figurine of calcite with radiocarbon date of 21,200 B.C. H. 8 cm.

FIG. 11. Modern and Neolithic images of a toad combined with a bud or flower. *1*, a wooden tomb marker from the cemetery of Nida, western Lithuania; *2*, Sesklo terra-cotta figurine, ca. 6000 B.C.

sign appears in association with sprouting seeds, pregnancy, and wherever the message of generation is accentuated.

The association of vulva, toad, and birth-giving posture is of particular importance because of its persistent continuity throughout prehistoric and historic times, up to our own century. There is a good deal of evidence, both folkloristic and historic (Egyptian, Greek, and Roman myths), that the toad is the Goddess herself and that she is also the vulva or uterus. Hence the belief in the "wandering womb" recorded in Egypt, in classical Greece, and still extant in European folklore.

In Lithuanian folklore, Ragana, the Goddess of Life and Death, now a witch, can change into a toad and cause death as well as birth. The toad in folklore is considered to have healing powers as well as venom. The portrayal of woman-toad hybrids is evidenced throughout the millennia and up to the twentieth century, usually exhibiting a supernatural vulva, as the examples from Bronze Age and modern Germany illustrate (fig. 9, 2, 3). It is interesting to observe on a modern ex-voto tablet from Catholic southern Germany the toad with a human vulva on its back next to the portrayal of the Virgin (fig. 9, 3). The toad as symbol of regeneration can be seen in the cemetery of Nida, western Lithuania, where many tombstones are in the form of a toad with a lily sprouting from its head (fig. 11, 1). The combination of a toad with a bud is attested as early as 6000 B.C. in Neolithic Greece (fig. 11, 2). In the Upper Palaeolithic, the association of vulvas with plants suggests a related symbolic content.

In summary, through the ages, the symbolism of the vulva, and particularly its association with the symbols of becoming— seeds, buds, sprouts, aquatic signs, pregnant bellies, and prominent buttocks—suggests that it was an image central to birth-giving and regeneration, an organic, not an erotic, symbol. The suggestion that unreal, exaggerated buttocks are symbolically related to the idea of germination or life promotion may on first consideration appear strange, but the long continuity of this configuration and its association with eggs, seeds, and other symbols of becoming is very persuasive.

Some scholars have thought that the large posteriors of the Palaeolithic and Neolithic figurines are intentionally pornographic (Absolon, 1949) or erotic (Onians, 1978). Others regarded them as barbaric ideals of beauty. It is my contention that it is the shape of a sculpture or engraving and the association of symbols, such as engraved or painted signs over the buttocks, that reveal its symbolic meaning. The associated symbolism of the egg or double-egg is attested in the European Copper Age, particularly by pictorial painting on Cucuteni vases of the early fourth millennium B.C. (fig. 12). The symbolic intention can be seen in the famous Perigordian-Gravettian "Venuses," their buttocks and breasts shaped like double-eggs. One of the best examples of this symbolism is the "Venus" from Lespugue, southern France (fig. 13). The "Venus" of Willendorf (not illustrated), those from Grimaldi in Italy (fig. 14) and Gagarino in Russia (fig. 15) are similarly shaped. Within the buttocks of one Magdalenian engraving is a circle, probably an egg (fig. 16). Hundreds, if not thousands, of Magdalenian, Neolithic, and later images with exaggerated posteriors reiterate again and again the cosmic myth of the Goddess as a water bird, carrying an egg or a double-egg in her body.

Variously abstracted female, human, and bird forms are continuous from the Magdalenian epoch through the Neolithic, Chalcolithic, and Copper Age; thus a series of Upper Palaeolithic figurines depicts nothing but the buttocks, the upper and lower parts of the body reduced to cones, and small carvings or pendants in the shape of buttocks or in double-egg form continue down to the Maltese culture of the fourth millennium B.C. In Cucutenian and Minoan art, the buttocks symbol became fused with the double-fruit symbol (fig. 17). In European folklore to this day, the symbol of a double-fruit, double-leaf, or double-ear signifies good luck and fertility.

LIFE-GIVING AND LIFE-TAKING

In her aspect as Life-giver, the Goddess is best represented as a female with exaggerated breasts or by breasts alone. The breasts

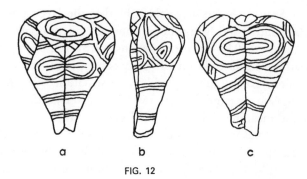

FIG. 12

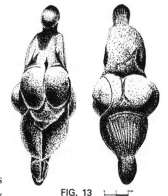

FIG. 12. Double-egg inside buttocks of terra-cotta figurine (broken below the waist), ca. 4500 B.C., Novye Ruseshty, Moldavia, Cucuteni-Tripolye culture. Note the symbolic decoration on exterior that repeats the double-egg motif. H. ca. 4 cm.

FIG. 13. The "Venus" of Lespugue, Haute-Garonne, Pyrenees, carved of mammoth ivory; ca. 24,000 B.C. Breasts, buttocks are a double-egg form. H. 14.7 cm.

FIG. 14. The "Venus" of Grimaldi (cave of Tunnel), carved of steatite, with double-egg buttocks, breasts, and pregnant belly. H. 6.1 cm.

FIG. 13

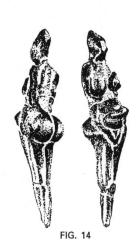

FIG. 14

38

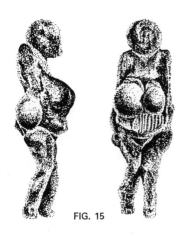

FIG. 15

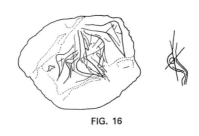

FIG. 16

FIG. 15. Ivory figurine from Gagarino, central Russia. Although found far from southern France and Italy, the figurine has egg-shaped buttocks, breasts, and pregnant belly. H. 12.7 cm.

FIG. 16. *1*, Late Magdalenian engraving of schematized female figure with egg inside the buttocks. The figure is crossed with two lines, probably representing magic, connected with the promotion of life. *2*, Engravings of "buttock figures" on a stone slab from La Roche at Lalinde, southern France.

FIG. 17

FIG. 17. Buttocks or double-fruit symbol painted in the central register of a Cucuteni vase (frequent motif of pictorial art of Old Europe). The upper register features a seed or vulva crossed by two lines and flanked by chevrons. Nedeia at Ghelaesti, Moldavia, northeastern Romania. Cucuteni B culture, date ca. 3800–3600 B.C.

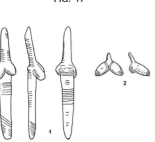

FIG. 18

FIG. 18. *1*, Schematized human figure with large breasts, incised with groups of parallel lines; *2*, pendant-bead in the form of breasts. Dolní Vestonice, Moravia, Czechoslovakia. East Gravettian, ca. 26,000 B.C. Carvings in mammoth tusk.

FIG. 19

FIG. 20

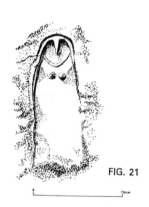

FIG. 21

FIG. 19. Female nude with pendulous breasts, wings, and bird head from Pech-Merle, Cabrerets, Lot, southern France. Cave wall finger-painting. H. approx. 70 cm. Probably Magdalenian (earlier considered to be of the Aurignacian epoch).

FIG. 20. Anthropomorphic vase with breasts and upraised arms (or feet). Decorated with snake-spiral design (lower register) and panels of meanders (upper register). Gradešnica, early Vinča site, northwestern Bulgaria. Date: ca. 5000–4500 B.C. H. 30 cm. Color: red with encrustation in white.

FIG. 21. The owl-faced Goddess of Death. Gravure on the wall at entrance to the rock-cut tomb. Coizard, Marne, France.

FIG. 22. Urn from Troy V (end of the third millennium B.C.) with an owl face on the lid and breasts; handles as wings.

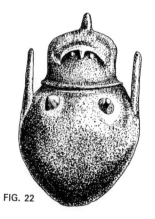

FIG. 22

were usually marked with parallel lines, chevrons, or crosses (whirls). Thus the celestial Breasts become an icon of the source of nourishment (milk or rain) or of life maintenance in general. The use of parallel lines and chevrons as symbolic marks on figurines occurs as early as the East Gravettian (Pavlovian) mammoth ivory carving from Dolni Vestonice in Moravia of ca. 26,000 B.C. (fig. 18, 1).

Only the breasts are naturalistically rendered on the abstract rod-shaped human figure; neither belly nor legs are indicated. The featureless head merges with the neck to form a single column, and groups of parallel lines are incised at the upper end of the rod and below the notched breasts.

From the same site, an even more abstract rendering of the female principle—the breasts alone—is an ivory pendant-bead in the pyramidal form of two breasts at the base of a conical neck (fig. 18, 2). The aspect of nourishing or life-giving is very early associated with the ornithomorphic shape of the Goddess. Bird-beaked "Venuses" in the Upper Palaeolithic cave of Pech-Merle, Lot, southern France, are finger-painted portrayals of female bodies with bird masks, wings, and pendulous breasts (fig. 18). Figures of the Goddess with large breasts and ornithomorphic features continued down to the Copper Age and, in some areas of Europe, into the Bronze and Iron Age.

After the invention of pottery, another symbolically related series appeared: the Goddess as the nourishing vessel. Such anthropomorphic or ornithomorphic vases have breasts and are marked with chevrons (Goddess sign) or with spirals, meanders, parallel lines, or streams (liquid sign; fig. 20).

The life-giving, nourishing Goddess with breasts appears in the form of menhirs or is engraved on slabs of megalithic tombs. The images range in western Europe from Italy to the British Isles, where they date from the fourth and third millennia B.C. In most cases, the sole attributes of the Goddess are simply breasts and a necklace. Occasionally, ornithomorphic features—eyes and browridges, apparently of an owl—are present, linking the megalithic Goddess with the archaic Bird Goddess (fig. 21). Her presence in connection with the megalithic tombs suggests that the same Goddess of Death aspect prototype of the ambiguous Fate Goddess of European mythologies is the apportioner of both good or bad in life and the determiner of its length. In European folklore, the owl is the bird of death; her appearance portends the end of life. The marble figurines deposited in Cycladic graves wear masks with owlish features; owl-shaped urns, or better said, urns in the shape of the Bird Goddess with owlish features, dating from the end of the fourth and early third millennia B.C. are known from Troy (fig. 22) and from the Baden culture of east central Europe (Hungary).

CONCLUSIONS

We have seen that there is ample evidence to support the hypothesis that the "monstrous Venus" of prehistory was one manifestation of a long-enduring tradition of cosmogonic myth as old, perhaps, as human culture. Its evolution may be seen in later forms even in historic times.

The "monstrous Venus" is a *religious* representation—the reification of the Life Genetrix. Those body parts which in our eyes seem exaggerated or grotesque are those parts of her which are most significant, magical, and sacred, the visible, productive source of cyclic life continuance. The images discussed in this article seem to be shapes of the life-generating Great Goddess in her various aspects and functions. The life-producing (generating) feature was not only the pregnant belly or the vulva but also buttocks and breasts—often depicted as double-eggs: She was Giver-of-All.

These functions were retained by the European Fate Goddess and other later, usually debased forms of the Goddesses of Life, Death, and Regeneration, still extant in the folklore of Christianized European peoples. Her epiphanies were many: she generally appeared as a human female but frequently as a water bird, snake, owl, toad, bear (and probably as she-bison in the Upper Palaeolithic). She was the more-than-human Mother. If the term *Great Mother* is used, it should be understood as *Universal Great*

42

Mother, whose powers pervade all nature, human life, the animal world, and all vegetation.

It is thus likely that goddess images were produced for the reenactment of seasonal communal and family rituals. After the rituals, they were probably kept for some time, to assure well-being. In Old Europe of 6500–3500 B.C., the figurines were kept on altars in domestic shrines, on oven platforms inside and outside the house, or in other places of cult activities. From the Upper Palaeolithic to the beginning of the patriarchal, Indo-European era in Europe (roughly to about 3000 B.C.), the worship of the Great Goddess was universal in Old Europe.

EDITORIAL NOTE

Marija Gimbutas's *Language of the Goddess,* which she had sent to me in manuscript form, is by any standards a signal contribution to the field.[1] The bibliography alone comprised sixty-nine pages of closely typed titles, and it had almost five hundred captioned illustrations. The original text was a typescript of three hundred and twenty-two pages.

When the author asked me to do a review, it was a doubly happy occasion for I respect her both as a path-breaking scholar and talented field-archaeologist as well as a friend of a decade. And I still recall our many conversations on symbols before the publication of her *Goddesses and Gods of Old Europe, 6500–3500 B.C.*[2] We discussed the existence of a very early symbolic-linguistic system, possibly along the structural lines of the Na-khi mnemonic system (to which I had been introduced by personal meetings with the late Joseph F. Rock).

"Symbols of the Goddess" would have been more accurate than "Language." The archaeology does not yet warrant the word language, which implies syntax and rules of word formation. The only attempt I know of by an archaeologist to establish a case for a language per se is that of Sean Winn, one of Marija Gimbutas' doctoral students, who now holds a professorship of his own. Though she references him in her bibliography, Gimbutas does not fully discuss his truly pioneering work in collecting a mass of symbols and arranging them in types.

In 1985 (on p.114f. of his *Destiny and Control*)* the present editor remarked on Winn's work and showed that his signs (and hence Gimbutas', since they worked from the same sites and sources) distilled down into twelve basic types which not only had definite symbols connecting with the ancient zodiacal signs and, even more anciently (and modernly!) with what are now called "phosphenes"—primordial visual images in the human mind which can be ellicited from the visual cortex of the brain.

We extensively commented on this tie-in and noted it to Marija who, however, was somewhat on the disinterested side where harder analytical science was concerned. But such blocks will have to be overcome by anyone who wants to understand the ancient symbols in a reasoned scientific context that would begin to explain their power objectively.

We also talked about chrysalids—a natural symbol of metamorphosis into a beautiful winged adult: the same reasoning that led the later Greeks and Aztecs independently to hit upon the butterfly ("flying flower" in Nahuatl) as the symbol of the human soul and its ultimate destiny. I noted then that the old chrysalis images often recall cicadas, jade images of which were used in ancient China as a symbol of regeneration and immortality.[3] Since the cicada exists in Europe as well as in China, the connection may well have been made between the similar processes that occur in the butterfly chrysalis and the cicada pupa. It is not by chance that the Ragana, the old Lithuanian image of the Great Goddess, has among her symbols both the butterfly and the cicada.

This work is not repetitive but is an encyclopedic synthesis of a wealth of valuable and often inaccessible illustrative material. It also represents a synthesis of her matured thinking on the subject.

---

*In three of the tables concerning the phosphenes the following printer's errors should be corrected. In Figure 4.3 (pp.110–111) the phosphene symbols should be turned upside down so that the bottom image on p.111 becomes the top one on p.110, the first, second and fourth columns of the Figure remaining unchanged. (Table 4.3, in pages 112–113, is correct.) In Table 4.5 (p.115) the first (left-hand) column should read downward 1,2,3,4; the third entry in the third column should read 7(>3.5); and the symbols in the last or fifth column should be reading downward: △,▽,△,▽.

The introduction and final chapter, which are really *tours de force,* can be profitably read first, as they will then orient the reader through a veritable Minoan (and older) labyrinth of pictographic and artifactual data from truly old horizons of time that stretch back millennia and that tree-ring and radiocarbon dating have helped to establish and sharpen, in one of the most exciting sagas of modern archaeology. But it is in the contents, significance, and meaning of those ramified ancient data that are our author's main concern. Her concern, however, is more authentic than any of the sexist platitudes could possibly be.

Whenever the theme of "goddess" arises in a still male-dominated culture such as our global one today, there is an inevitable sexual reaction on the part of that culture and of male commentators in particular—a reaction that does not desist even from unscholarly smirking and besmirching, with consequent denigrating effect.

Some years ago, Gimbutas published sharp and well-taken rejoinder to the smirk-and-leer theory that would reduce the ancient goddesses to simply sex symbols. In her deliberately entitled paper "Vulvas, Breasts, and Buttocks of the Goddess Creatress," she rebutted John Onians as a typical example of the smirk-besmirch school of thought on the Goddess.[4] Gimbutas correctly showed that the Goddess was primarily a life-giver, a source of new life and nourishment—and proved her point in a multitude of ways that all enabled us to understand the not sex-guilt-ridden mentality of the old peoples. They were not naive either. They simply were naturally and rightly awestruck by the mystery of the bringing forth and nurturing of new life: a function peculiarly feminine.

There was no guilt there. This attitude is well preserved in ancient Egyptian, where glyphs for vulva and phallus are commonplace in the holy writings used by both priestesses and priests in the most sacred and reverential contexts—without any of the guilty prurience of current culture, so astutely perceived by Freud and elaborated by him into a pathological mythology applied to our too prevalent psychic disorders. But his whole approach was incurably culture-bound and anthropologically provincial.

45

Gimbutas's writings have the ancient purity and objectivity of observation and intent and are a refreshing and healthy source of inspiration for young scholars. An apt summing up is found in the words of Nicholas Seare's 1983 *Rude Tales and Glorious.* "It is instructive to note that the Great Freedom from Good Taste that characterizes the modern era is limited to but one of the biological functions, the one that has been snickered at since the invention of sin."[5]

One need only regard the great contrast to those pilloried by Seare, in the sensitivity and authenticity of Diane Wolkstein's treatment of a similar theme in her book on the great Sumero-Babylonian Goddess Inanna,[6] which she wrote in collaboration with cuneiformist Samuel Noah Kramer, whose *From the Tablets of Sumer* (later, in 1981, republished more flamboyantly as *History Begins at Sumer*)[7] I first launched after having had the pleasurable editorial task of selecting it for publication. Also to be noted is that the studies of Diane Wolkstein and an earlier female commentator on Inanna, Judith Ochshorn,[8] are authentically based on the known legend translated by W. W. Hallo and J. J. van Dijk in 1968,[9] after which appeared S. N. Kramer's *The Sacred Marriage Rite* concerned with the same ancient Goddess, Inanna.[10] She—it is too often not realized or perceived—survived in the Babylonian Ishtar, the ancient Germanic Oster (which became our word *Easter*), and the Greek Astarte.

The contents of Gimbutas's book range far in time, space, and theme, for the Goddess our author addresses was a universal one and herself addressed the multiple variety of human, natural, and cosmic themes found symbolized in the earliest pottery and cultic vessel decorations, on seals, in spindle whorls, plaques, ritual objects, pendants, stelae, megalithic tombs, amulets, masks, and figurines. The continuity of the themes and ideas beyond these representations is then traced through later folklore into subsequent Indo-European and Christian times. The author should expand this sketch in a later book.

In the author's own words from the introduction to her original manuscript sent to the present editor:

The core of illustrations reproduced in this work dates from the period between 6500 and 3500 B.C. in southeastern Europe, and from c. 4500 to 2500 B.C. in western Europe. (The Neolithic started considerably later in the west.) Examples from the Upper Paleolithic are also introduced to demonstrate the origin and amazing longevity of certain images and signs: in some cases they go back to the Aurignacian period, c. 30,000 B.C.

However, the persistence of upper paleolithic/mesolithic/neolithic motifs in the Bronze Age is not ignored. In fact, being more articulate than their predecessors and full of life-affirming grace, the images and symbols of Bronze Age Cyprus, Crete, Thera, Sardinia, Sicily, and Malta are magnificent sources for our purpose. We shall make generous use of examples from these islands, especially Minoan Crete, before they were touched by Indo-European influences. Much of this great artistic culture lived on in ancient Greece and Rome and was inherited by Western civilization.

Beliefs concerning birth and death, sterility and fertility, the cyclicity of nature, the fragility of life and the constant threat of destruction, and the periodic need to secure the renewal of the generative process of nature are among the most conservative. With roots deep in prehistory, they live on, as do very archaic aspects of the prehistoric Goddess, in spite of the continuous process of erosion in the historic era. Passed on by the grandmothers and mothers of the European family, the ancient beliefs survived the superimposition of the Indo-European and finally the Christian mythical systems. The Goddess-centered religion existed for an enormous length of time, leaving an indelible imprint on the Western psyche.

The ancient symbols and beliefs that were recorded in historical times or those that are still extant in rural and peripheral areas of Europe—particularly in Basque, Breton, Welsh, Irish, Scottish, Baltic (Lithuanian and Latvian) and Slavic countries—are essential to the understanding of prehistoric symbols, since these later versions are known to us within their ritual and mythic contexts.

It is hoped that this work will open avenues to folklore treasures as a source for the reconstruction of prehistoric ideology. *Archaeofolklore* is a field as yet unexplored by archaeologists (and *vice versa:* rich archaeological sources are hardly touched by folklorists or mythologists) in spite of enormous possibilities.

Of great interest is her stratigraphy of ancient religious symbols, together with her richly substantiated tracing of the continuity of such symbols from Upper Paleolithic times. Only around 3500 B.C., with the invasion of southeastern Europe by patrilinear peoples, did the old goddess symbol system suffer radical change.

The sheep was the earliest domesticated animal, and the ram in early Neolithic times became a theriomorphic symbol associated with the universal Goddess, together with the wool/fleece symbol associated with her spinning and weaving of the fabric of all forms of life and the universe, together with all their associated tapestries of destiny.

It is important, in the light of our prior observations on the remarkable work under review, that death symbols in this most ancient religion were subordinated to those of life and regeneration. This old reasoning is quite philosophically sound: if death was the ultimate ruler of the cosmos, life would not be so abundantly persistent and prolific. Therefore, the old wisdom taught, it was life and not death that was primal. Indeed, the Copper Age (ca. 4500 B.C.) death-forms of the Goddess are themselves incorporated with regenerative symbols: at the very heart of death is life.

What is perhaps not clear enough in the author's presentation is that the regeneration doctrine of the ancient religion was not the unsatisfying generalization "you will die but the constituents of your body will be used for some other life form." We must recall that the widespread chrysalid symbol depicts a quite different idea: the *individual* regeneration of a *particular* larva that, having self-transformed into a specific pupa or chrysalid, then again self-transmutes into its adult or imago form capable of free flight. The process is not one of de-individualization but of intensified and renewed individual existence.

The text under review should make it clearer that the Goddess "who needs [human] blood to create anew" is a later and degenerated form of the earliest religion in which life, not death, lay at the core of things. In fact, it is still insufficiently recognized that the cruel and ignorant cults of blood sacrifice—human or not—are always later degenerations of an earlier and much higher doctrine.[11] The modern religions that bless inhumane wars as "proofs of God's judgments" belong in the same late and degenerative cultic category that has pulled humanity down for millennia.

We hypocritically condemn ritual killers like the "Manson family" while condoning the same monstrous behavior politically on a mass scale. We had better recall the ancient teaching (in Egypt *par excellence*) of the sacredness of individual life and its temporary restriction and constriction in a "pupal" chamber of miraculous transformation. We must remember with Marija Gimbutas that "Celebration of Life is the leading motif in Old European ideology and art. . . . There was no simple death, only death *and* regeneration."

However, as Margaret Murray and Charles Godfrey Leland independently observed, and as Gimbutas again notes from new and rich evidence, "the Goddess religion went underground"—a process that began in the mid-fourth millennium before our era. Yet let us remember that until comparatively recently the standing stones and menhirs of Old Lithuania were called "goddesses" by folk traditionalists (cf. Gimbutas). But there was a price to be paid for this. As Gimbutas sums up:

> The Goddess gradually retreated. . . . Human alienation from the vital roots of earthly life ensued, the results of which are clear in our contemporary society. But the cycles never stop turning, and now we find the Goddess reemerging . . . bringing us hope for the future. . . .

At the end of her text, Gimbutas quotes one of this writer's favorite passages from Lucius Apuleius's vision of the universal Goddess Isis, who has invoked her as the Blessèd Queen of Heaven (cf. the derivative Christian appellation of the Divine Virgin as *Regina Coeli*). Then Isis speaks to him and says, in part,

> Behold, Lucius, I am come . . . I the true mother of all things, mistress of all divine powers, manifesting under one form all other gods and goddesses. At my will the celestial bodies move

through the heavens, and the winds and yea, the abysses of hell are commanded. My divinity is worshipped by many peoples under different names.

[The original reads "deorum dearumque facies uniformis," and is rightly emphasized in the text by Marija Gimbutas.]

Let us recall that Western scholarly attention began to be paid to the Great Goddess as far back as Johann J. Bachofen's work in the nineteenth century, principally his *Matriarchy and Primordial Religion* (1861).[12] Limited as that was by the then archaeological and anthropological horizons, it was a beginning—a beginning that was advanced by a major though still obscure figure in ancient folklore, myth, symbolism, and the archaeology of the Goddess, the late Herman Wirth (d. 1981), lecturer at the University of Augsburg in 1980 and former professor in ancient European culture and history at Leipzig and Berlin. Wirth anticipated much later work, and because his is insufficiently known, he merits mention here.

He saw the primordial Mother Goddess as the original religious impulse of humanity and, like Bachofen, regarded matriarchy as the earliest form of human society. He held that a resurgence of this impulse is now necessary, based on spiritual potential rather than external power, if our humanity is to survive. His prime value to the present study is that his archaeological research and symbolic analysis of artifacts led him to conclude that a universal Mother Goddess was worshiped long before a universal Father God.

One of his landmark papers (appearing in the Münster *Journal for Religious Science*) was entitled "The Symbolic-Historic Method."[13] In it he devoted great attention to archaic egg symbolism devolving about rebirth and regeneration, citing Louise Hagberg's little known "Easter Eggs and their pre-Christian Origin" (Fataburen, 1906), as well as the archaeologically unearthed Orphic inscription (made famous by Jane Harrison) *Gès pais eimi kai uranou asteroentos, autar emoi genos uraniōn:* "I am child of the Earth and the Starry Heaven, but my race is of Heaven alone." He also there discusses the egg-formed tomb-vase of

Kyrene, in connection with Orphic origins and the Mother Goddess as source of all eggs and seeds.

In the same paper, Wirth cites the too little known work of Franz Hančar, "On the Problem of the Venus-statuettes in the Eurasian Paleolithic" (*Praehistorische Zeitschrift,* 30–31, 1939–40: 128), citing Hančar's astute observation of "the well-developed meander ornaments on obviously cultic bird-figures, cut on mammoth ivory with unbelievable finesse and skill." Wirth then comments in the following words, so remarkably anticipating later work in the field: "These cultic birds with their symbolic ornaments are the same companion birds of a fully stylized statuette of the Great Mother-Goddess, the 'Stara Baba' [i.e., "Ancient Mother." *C.M.*] of Siberia as found at Kostyenki and Gagarino in the Don region, as well as around Willendorf in lower Austria: statuettes related also to the southwestern mother-goddess statues of Menton, Brassempouy and Laussel."

But Wirth goes farther than even ancient anthropology, and his aim is actually archaic linguistics. He seeks to unravel the symbolic ideographic repertoire, as revealed by Old European archaeology, into an at least partial reconstruction of the ideational life of those primeval cultures. The interested reader is referred to his *Universal Mother* published in 1974 at Marburg, which has as subtitle "The Discovery of the 'Old Italic' Inscriptions in the Palatinate Region, and Their Meaning."[14] In that work (p. 31) he discusses, among other things, the beak or "long nose" of depictions of the Goddess and its significance.

To find anyone else at this level of sophistication in this field, one must read Gimbutas. Another thing he shares with her is his fund of rich illustrative material; and it is a pity these two pioneering contributors to our knowledge of the ancient goddess religion did not meet before Wirth's passing in 1981 at the age of ninety-four. The writer, too, learned of him only afterward. But at least we can introduce them now, both mutually and to their readers.

With the work of Marija Gimbutas, the religion of Goddess rests on at least as scientific a footing as the religion of God. To see that the Goddess is not neglected today even in institutionalized Western culture, one need only glance at *The Virgin Mary in the*

Teaching of the Popes, published by the monks of Solesmes in France in 1981.[15] The Blessèd Damozel, "Queen of Heaven," *Regina Coeli,* the ancient hieroglyphic title of Isis,[16] still reigns.

Editor's Notes

1. M. Gimbutas, *Language of the Goddess* (San Francisco: HarperCollins, 1989). Page numbers for the following quotations from this book will be given in parentheses following each quotation.

2. M. Gimbutas. *Goddesses and Gods of Old Europe, 6500–3500 B.C.* (Berkeley and Los Angeles: University of California Press, 1982.) The first edition (1974) appeared as *Gods and Goddesses of Old Europe, 7000–3500 B.C.* Although rich inferences can be made for Neolithic agriculture in southeastern Europe as far back as 6700 B.C. (it occurred in northern Europe some three thousand years later), firm and abundant artifacts occur for 6500 B.C., the *terminus à quo* used in the second edition. The dates are based on dendrochronological analysis—tree-ring dating—now known to be very accurate and more dependable than radiocarbon dating used alone. Those interested in specifics of "the language of the Goddess" should consult the careful work of Shan Milton McChesney Winn, a student of Professor Gimbutas and now a professor in his own right. See in particular his *Signs of the Vinča Culture* (1981), cited on p. 114 of *Destiny and Control* (Musès 1985).

3. B. Laufer, *Jade* (New York: Dover, 1974), 299–301.

4. M. Gimbutas, "Vulvas, Breasts and Buttocks of the Goddess Creatress," in *Studies in Honor of Franklin D. Murphy,* (Los Angeles: Institute of Archaeology, UCLA, 1981), 15–42.

5. Nicholas Seare, *Rude Tales and Glorious,* (New York: C. N. Potter Publishing, 1983), xiii–xiv.

6. D. Wolkstein and S. N. Kramer, *Inanna, Queen of Heaven and Earth* (New York: Harper & Row, 1983).

7. An assertion to which I have always demurred on scientific grounds and for that reason published the first (1958) edition of my old colleague Sam Kramer's book using the more legitimate title *From the Tablets of Sumer,* the Doubleday paperback edition of which led directly to the second hardback edition by another house. Those publishers were evidently not too squeamish about an inaccurate title that might sell more books. Nonetheless, *From the Tablets of Sumer* is the book from which the latter twentieth-century era of archaeological best-sellers can be dated.

8. J. Ochshorn, *The Female Experience and the Nature of the Divine* (Bloomington: Indiana University Press, 1981), 87–88, 121ff.

9. W. W. Hallo and J. J. van Dijk, trans., *The Exaltation of Inanna* (New Haven: Yale University Press, 1968).

10. S. N. Kramer, *The Sacred Marriage Rite* (Bloomington: University of Indiana Press, 1969).

11. Some recent speculations attempting to derive later blood sacrifice from "maybe" Paleolithic male "hunting ritual" are so unsubstantiated or evidentially counterindicated as not to merit more than summary mention here. As that great scholar Ananda Coomaraswamy perceived as early as 1935, "Nor can it be doubted that a cult of the One Madonna existed already in the Paleolithic age" (*The R̥g Veda as Land Náma-Bók*, p. 2 of introduction).

12. J. J. Bachofen, *Gesammelte Werke,* edited by K. Meuli et al. (Basel, 1948), and *Mutterrecht und Urreligion,* first appeared in 1861 and was later republished at Leipzig in 1927.

13. H. Wirth, "Die Symbolhistorische Methode," *Ztschr. f. Religionswissenschaft* (Münster, Westfalen), (1955).

14. H. Wirth, *Allmutter* (Marburg and der Lahn, 1974). This work is still obtainable from Monsieur Andreas Lentz, 82 Weislingen, F–67290 Wingen-sur-Moder, France.

15. Moines de Solesmes, *La Vierge Marie dans l'Enseignement des Papes* (Sablé-sur-Sarthe, France: Abbaye Saint Pierre de Solesmes), 1981.

16. Nb • t p • t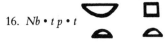

References

Gimbutas, M. *Comparative Civilizations Review,* Fall 1981.

Gimbutas, M. *The Gods and Goddesses of Old Europe, 7000–3500 B.C. Myths, Legends and Cult Images.* London: Thames and Hudson, 1974. University of California Press, 1982, 2d and updated ed.

Hancăr, F. Problem der Venusstatuetten im eurasiatischen *Jungpalaeolithikum. Prähistorische Zeitschrift* 30–31. Berlin, 1940.

Leroi-Gourhan, A. *The Treasures of Prehistoric Art.* New York: Abrams, 1967.

Luquet, G.-H. Les Venus paléolithiques. *Journal de Psychologie* (Paris) 31 (1934).

Marshack, A. *The Roots of Civilization.* New York: MacGraw-Hill, 1972.

Pales, L. Les ci-devant Venus stéatopyges aurignaciennes. *Simposium Internacional de Arte Rupestre.* Santander, 1968.

Passemard, L. *Les statuettes féminines paléolithiques dites Venus stéatopyges.* Nimes: Teissier, 1933.

Piette, E. *L'art pendant l'âge du renne.* Paris: Masson, 1907.

Saccasyn dalla Santa, E. *Les figures humaines du Paléolithique supérior.* Anvers: De Sikkel, 1947.

3

THE MYSTERY NUMBER
OF THE GODDESS

JOSEPH CAMPBELL

ALL THINGS ANEW

As prophesied in *The Poetic Edda,*

> Five hundred and forty doors there are,
>   I ween, in Valhall's walls;
> Eight hundred fighters through each door fare
>   When to war with the Wolf they go.[1]

$540 \times 800 = 432,000$, which in the Hindu Purāṇas, or "Chronicles of Ancient Lore," is the number of years reckoned to the Kali Yuga, the present cycle of time, which is to be the last and shortest of four cycles that together compose a "Great Cycle" or Mahāyuga of 4,320,000 years, which is to end in a universal flood.

The Purāṇas date from ca. A.D. 400 to 1000; the Eddic verses from ca. A.D. 900 to 1100. The obvious question to be asked, therefore, is, By what coincidence can this number have appeared both in India and in Iceland in association with a mythology of recurrent cycles of time? For as told further in the Eddas,

> Now do I see the earth anew
> Rise all green from the waves again;
> The cataracts fall, and the eagle flies,
> And fish he catches beneath the cliffs.
>
> In wondrous beauty once again
> Shall the golden tables stand mid the grass,
> Which the gods owned in days of old.

The fields unsowed bear ripened fruit,
All ills grow better, and Baldr comes back;
Baldr and Hoth dwell in Hropt's battle-hall,
And the mighty gods.[2]

One cannot but think of the prophesied Day of Doom of the New Testament (Mark 13), which, according to Rev. 21:1, is to be followed by "a new heaven and new earth; for the first heaven and the first earth had passed away, and the sea was no more." Can the number 432 have been associated with this biblical cycle as well as with the Hindu cycle and the Norse? We read further in the book of the revelation beheld on the Greek island of Patmos by St. John:

> Then came one of the seven angels who had the seven bowls full of the seven last plagues, and spoke to me, saying: "Come, I will show you *the Bride, the wife of the Lamb*." And in the Spirit he carried me away to a great, high mountain, and showed me the holy city Jerusalem coming down out of heaven from God, having the glory of God, its radiance like a most rare jewel, like a jasper, clear as crystal. It had a great, high wall, with twelve gates, and at the gates twelve angels, and on the gates the names of the twelve tribes of the sons of Israel were inscribed; on the east three gates, on the north three gates, on the south three gates, and on the west three gates. And the wall of the city had twelve foundations, and on them the twelve names of the twelve apostles of the Lamb.
>
> And he who talked with me had a measuring rod of gold to measure the city and its gates and walls. *The city lies foursquare, its length the same as its breadth, and he measured the city with his rod, twelve thousand stadia; its length and breadth and height are equal.* He also measured its wall, a hundred and forty-four cubits by a man's measure, that is, an angel's. The wall was built of jasper, while the city was of pure gold, clear as glass. . . . And the twelve gates were twelve pearls, each of the gates made of a single pearl, and the street of the city was pure gold, transparent as glass. (Rev. 21:9–21, abridged, the italics, of course, are mine)

$12,000 \times 12,000 \times 12,000$ stadia $= 1,728$ billion cubic stadia, which, when divided by 4, equals 432 billion.[3] Moreover, in Rev. 13:18 it is declared that the number of the name of the "beast rising out of the sea, with ten horns and seven heads, with ten diadems upon its horns and a blasphemous name upon its heads" (Rev. 13:1), is 666; whereas 6 × 6 × 6 = 216, which is half of 432.

The earliest known appearance of this number was in the writings of a Chaldean priest of the god Marduk, Berossos, who, ca. 280 B.C. composed in Greek a synopsis of Babylonian myth and history in which it was reported that, between the legendary date of the "descent of kingship" on the early Sumerian city of Kish and the coming of the mythological flood, ten kings ruled in Sumer through a period of 432,000 years. The universal flood there reported is the same as that of Genesis 6–7, of which the earliest known account has been found on a very greatly damaged cuneiform tablet from the ruins of Nippur, of a date ca. 2000 B.C.[4] There the ancient tale is told of a pious king Ziusudra, last of the line of ten long-lived antediluvian monarchs of the city of Shuruppak, who, while standing by a wall, heard a voice advising him to build himself an ark.

The . . . place . . .
The people . . .
A rainstorm . . .
At that time [the Goddess] Nintu screamed like a woman
      in travail
The pure [Goddess] Inanna wailed because of her people.
[The God] Enki in his heart took counsel.
[The Great Gods] An, Enlil, Enki and [the Goddess] Ninhursag.
The gods of heaven and earth invoked the names of An and Enlil.

Ziusudra at that time was king, the lustral priest of . . .
He built a huge . . .
Humbly prostrating himself, reverently . . .
Daily and perseveringly standing in attendance . . .
Auguring by dreams, such as never were seen before . . .
Conjuring in the name of heaven and earth . . .

      . . . the gods, a wall . . .
Ziusudra, standing at its side, heard:
    "At the wall, at my left hand stand . . .
    At the wall, I would speak to thee a word.
    O my holy one, open thine ear to me.

"By our hand a rainstorm . . . will be sent,
To destroy the seed of mankind . . .
Is the decision, the word of the assembly of the gods,
The command of An and Enlil . . .
Its kingdom . . . its rule . . .

All the windstorms of immense power, they all came together.
The rainstorm . . . raged along with them.
And when for seven days and seven nights
The rainstorm in the land had raged,
The huge boat on the great waters by the windstorm had been
    carried away.
Utu, the sun came forth, shedding light over heaven and earth.

Ziusudra opened a window of the huge boat.
He let the light of the sun-god, the hero, come into the
    interior of the huge boat.
Ziusudra, the king,
Prostrated himself before Utu.
The king: he sacrifices an ox, slaughters a sheep.

"By the soul of heaven, by the soul of earth, do ye conjure
    him, that he may . . . with you.
By the soul of heaven, by the soul of earth, O An and
    Enlil, do ye conjure and he will . . . with you."

Vegetation, coming out of the earth, rises.
Ziusudra, the king,
Before An and Enlil prostrates himself.
Life like that of a god they bestow on him.
An eternal soul like that of a god they create for him.
Whereupon Ziusudra, the king,
Bearing the title, "Preserver of the Seed of Mankind,"
On a . . . mountain, the mountain of Dilmun, they caused
    to dwell . . .[5]

Returning to the Bible, we find that, in Genesis 5, ten antediluvian patriarchs are named from Adam to Noah; the first, of course, being Adam, who, as we read, "when he had lived 130 years became the father of a son . . . and named him Seth." Continuing: "When Seth had lived 105 years, he became the father of Enosh . . ." And likewise: "When Enosh had lived 90 years, he became the father of Kenon. . . . When Kenon had lived 70 years, he became the father of Mahalalel," and so on, to, "When Lamech had lived 182 years, he became the father of a son, and called his name Noah. . . ." Following all of which, we learn from Gen. 7:6 that "Noah was 600 years old when the flood of waters came upon the earth."

Comparing this remarkable genealogical fantasy with Berossos's equally bizarre list of the years of reign of the antediluvian kings, and totaling the two sums, we find as follows:

Berossos		Genesis 5 and 7:6	
Antediluvian kings	*Years of reign*	*Antediluvian patriarchs*	*Years to begetting of sons*
1. Aloros	36,000	Adam	130
2. Alaparos	10,800	Seth	105
3. Amelon	46,800	Enosh	90
4. Ammenon	43,200	Kenon	70
5. Megalaros	64,800	Mahalalel	65
6. Daonos	36,000	Jared	162
7. Eudoraches	64,800	Enoch	65
8. Amempsinos	36,000	Methuselah	187
9. Opartes	28,800	Lamech	182
10. Xisuthros	64,800	Noah, yrs. to flood:	600
[= Ziusudra]	432,000		1,656

Between the totals of Berossos and the compilers of Genesis 5–7, there is apparently an irreconcilable difference. However, as demonstrated over a century ago in a paper, "The Dates of Genesis," by the distinguished Jewish Assyriologist Julius Oppert, who in his day was known as the "Nestor of Assyriology,"[6] both totals contain 72 as a factor, this being the number of years required in the precession of the equinoxes for an advance of 1 degree along the zodiac. 432,000 divided by 72 = 6,000, while 1656 divided by 72 = 23. So that the relationship is of 6,000 to 23. But in the Jewish calendar, one year is reckoned as of 365 days, which number in 23 years, plus the 5 leap-year days of that period, amounts to 8,400 days, or 1,200 seven-day weeks; which last sum, multiplied by 72, to find *the number of seven-day weeks in 23 × 72 = 1,656 years,* yields 1,200 × 72 = 86,400, which is twice 43,200.

So that in the Book of Genesis two distinct theologies have been now revealed. The first is that of the usually recognized, personal Creator-God of Abraham, Isaac, and Jacob, who saw that "the wickedness of man was great in the earth . . . and was sorry that he had made man on the earth, and it grieved him to his heart. So the Lord said, 'I will blot out man whom I have created from the face of the ground, man and beast and creeping things and birds of the air, for I am sorry that I have made them'" (Gen. 6:5–7). Whereas the other, very different theology has been hidden all these years beneath the elaborately disguised number 86,400, which can be only a covert reference to the mathematically governed Gentile cosmology preserved to this day in the Hindu Purāṇas, of an unending series of cycles of world appearances and dissolutions, the latter following inevitably upon the former, not because of any god's disappointment in his creation, but as night follows day.

For the Jews, it will be recalled, had been for fifty years exiled from their own capital to Babylon (586–539 B.C.), and the priestly hands that compiled the genealogical schedule of Genesis, chapter 5—so nicely contrived to join the 600 years of Noah's age at the time of the Flood, as reported in chapter 7, to produce a total exactly of 1,656—were of a postexilic generation and contemporaries approximately of Berossos, the famous Chaldean priest.

THE GODDESS UNIVERSE

But already in the mangled cuneiform Flood text above, quoted from ca. 2000 B.C., the signs are discernable of at least two distinct orders of mythology. For in Sumerian terms, that text was very late, and during the course of a preceding culture-history of no less than 1500 years, the founding cosmological insight represented in the Flood legend had become overlaid by folkloristic layerings of imaginative, anecdotal narrative. Throughout those very greatly troubled times the land of Sumer had been open to both peaceful settlement and violent invasions by Semitic hordes from the Syro-Arabian desert,[7] until finally, ca. 2350 B.C., the mighty usurper, Sargon I of Akkad, carved out for himself with great violence and destruction—of which his monuments proudly boast—an empire that extended from the Taurus ranges to the Persian Gulf, which "began," as Samuel Noah Kramer has remarked, "the Semitization of Sumer that finally brought about the end of the Sumerian people, at least as an identifiable political and ethnic entity. . . . His influence made itself felt in one way or another from Egypt to India."[8]

The mutilated Flood text of ca. 2000 B.C. is from the ruins of Nippur, which Sargon's grandson, Naram-Sin, sacked and desecrated ca. 2230 B.C. The Sargonids themselves were then overpowered, ca. 2150 B.C., by a mountain people from the Zagros range, the Guti, who overran the empire and maintained control in Mesopotamia until ca. 2050 B.C., when Utuhegel of Erech, a Sumerian, overthrew their king Tirigan and, having caused him to be blinded and brought before his throne, "set his foot upon his neck."[9]

The following century, which is that of our Flood text and known to scholarship as Dynasty III of Ur (ca. 2050–1950 B.C.), was an immensely productive season of renewed Sumerian achievement in the arts, in temple building, religious reconstruction, and text recording. Indeed, practically all that we now know of the literature, mythology, and culture of this remarkable, first literate people in the history of civilization dates from the monuments of this one brief but very precious Sumerian century. A resurgent, reconstructed civilization, however, is not the same as an originating, form-envisioning culture; 350 years of alien domination cannot be written away. As Kramer has described the condition of the material of which he has been the leading modern translator:

> Intellectually speaking, the Sumerian myths reveal a rather mature and sophisticated approach to the gods and their divine activities; behind them can be recognized considerable cosmological and theological reflection. By and large, however, the Sumerian mythographers were the direct heirs of the illiterate minstrels and bards of earlier days, and their first aim was to compose narrative poems about the gods that would be appealing, inspiring, and entertaining. Their main literary tools were

not logic and reason but imagination and fantasy. In telling their stories they did not hesitate to invent motives and incidents patterned on human action that could not possibly have any basis in rational and speculative thought. Nor did they hesitate to adopt legendary and folkloristic motifs that had nothing to do with cosmological inquiry and inference.

As yet, no Sumerian myths have been recovered dealing directly and explicitly with the creation of the universe; what little is known about the Sumerian cosmogonic ideas has been inferred from laconic statements scattered throughout the literary documents. But we do have a number of myths concerned with the organization of the universe and its cultural processes, the creation of man, and the establishment of civilization.[10]

Prehistorically, the Sumerians were not aboriginal to Mesopotamia. Their native heath is unknown. Speaking an agglutinative tongue showing affinities, on one hand, with the Uralo-Altaic languages (Balto-Finnish, Hungarian, Volgaic, Uralien, Samoyedic, Turkish, Mongolian, and Eskimo)[11] and, on the other hand, with the Dravidian tongues of India, the Pelasgian of pre-Homeric Greece, Georgian of the Caucasus, and Basque of the Pyrenees,[12] they had arrived apparently ca. 3500 B.C. to find the river lands already occupied by an advanced Neolithic, farming and cattle-raising population known to science as the Ubaidian (also, Proto-Euphratean), who, as Kramer tells, were "the first important civilizing force in ancient Sumer, its first farmers, cultivators, cattle-raisers, and fishermen; its first weavers, leatherworkers, carpenters, smiths, potters, and masons."[13] The culture stage represented was that of Marija Gimbutas's *The Goddesses and Gods of Old Europe, 7000–3500 B.C.*, where the paramount divinity of eastern Europe in that period is shown to have been (to quote Gimbutas's characterization) "the Great Goddess of Life, Death and Regeneration in anthropomorphic form with a projection of her powers through insects and animals."[14] "As a supreme Creator who creates from her own substance," states Gimbutas, "she is the primary goddess of the old European pantheon." And further: "Because her main function was to regenerate life forces, the goddess was flanked by male animals noted for their physical strength. . . . The European Great Goddess, like the Sumerian Ninkhursag, gave life to the dead."[15]

The elegance of the grade of civilization represented in the remains of this Mother Goddess culture-stratum in all of its appearances, whether in the Old Europe of Marija Gimbutas's revelations, the late Neolithic and Chalcolithic sites of Anatolia and the Near East, or in the pre-Harappan strata of Neolithic northwest India, gives evidence to the bold suggestion of Alain Daniélou in his recently published comparative study of the religions of Shiva and Dionysus, of a single "great cultural movement extending from India to Portugal,"[16] dating from the sixth millennium B.C., and documented, not in scripture (since there was no writing at that time), but in the grace and clarity of its visual arts. For the ambience is strongly female: exemplary of a profoundly felt, inward knowledge of the transpersonal imperatives and quality of life, to which expression is given in visual art as a cosmetic or accenting adornment, not only of the person, but of anything of significance to life in the culture.

It is this joy in the beautification of life that especially marks the monuments of this earliest agricultural stage; and everywhere its paramount divinity is that metaphoric apparition of the life that outlives death who became in later centuries venerated as the Goddess of Many Names. "I am she," she declared, for example, on appearing as Queen Isis before her devotee Lucius Apuleius at the conclusion of the ordeal described in his allegorical picaresque novel, *The Golden Ass* (second century A.D.):

> I am she that is the natural mother of all things, mistress and governess of all the elements, the initial progeny of worlds, chief of the powers divine, queen of all that are in hell, the principal of them that dwell in heaven, manifested alone and under one form of all the gods and goddesses. At my will the planets of the sky, the wholesome winds of the seas, and the lamentable silences of hell are disposed; my name, my divinity is adored throughout the world, in divers manners, in variable customs, and by many names.
>
> For the Phrygians that are the first of all men call me the Mother of the gods of Pessinus; the Athenians, which are sprung

from their own soil, Cecropian Minerva; the Cyprians, which are girt about by the sea, Paphian Venus; the Cretans, which bear arrows, Dictynian Diana; the Sicilians, which speak three tongues, infernal Proserpine; the Eleusinians, their ancient goddess Ceres; some Juno, others Bellona, others Hecate, others Ramnusiee, and principally both sort of Ethiopians, which dwell in the Orient and are enlightened by the morning rays of the sun; and the Egyptians, which are excellent in all kind of ancient doctrine, and by their proper ceremonies accustomed to worship me, do call me by my true name, Queen Isis.

Behold I am come to take pity on thy fortune and tribulation; behold I am present to favor and aid thee; leave off thy weeping and lamentation, put away all thy sorrow, for behold the healthful day which is ordained by my providence.[17]

On a gold signet ring from Minoan Crete, ca. 2000–1500 B.C., the Goddess appears standing in majesty on a mountaintop, holding in her extended hand the staff or scepter of authority. Her equivalent form in Sumer at that time was Ninhursag, named in the Flood legend above quoted. "Her name," as Samuel Kramer remarks, "may originally have been Ki '(mother) Earth,' and she was probably taken to be the consort of An, 'Heaven,'—An and Ki thus may have been conceived as the parents of all the gods. She was also known as Nintu, 'the lady who gave birth.'"[18]

In a celestial manifestation, the Goddess was known to the Sumerians in the person also of the pure and lovely Inanna (likewise named in the Flood text), who from heaven descended through seven gates to the netherworld to bring the dead to eternal life. In later Semitic myths, she is Ishtar, descending to the underworld to restore life to her beloved Tammuz, and in the Hellenized-Semitic Christian heritage her part is played by Christ in the episode, following the Crucifixion, of his "Harrowing of Hell," when, shattering the infernal gates, he "descended into hell," there to rescue to eternal life the prophets and justified of the Old Testament (leaving, however, the Greeks and Romans, Socrates, Plato, Aristotle, Virgil, Cato, Horace, and the rest, in the devil's keep).

FIG. 1. Goddess of the World Mountain. Design from a gold signet ring. Knossos, Crete, ca. 1500 B.C. From Sir Arthur Evans, *The Palace of Minos,* 4 vols. (1921–36).

There were many variants of the adventure represented in the vast amalgam of analogous mythologies brought together and compounded during the period immediately following the conquests of Alexander: Egyptian Isis searching to resurrect the remains of Osiris, her dismembered lord; Eleusinian Demeter seeking to recover her abducted child, Persephone; Aphrodite and Adonis; Babylonian Ishtar and Tammuz. In India, the model was the bride of Shiva, Satī (pronounced Suttee), whose role was to be enacted, until forbidden by British law in 1829, by every widowed wife following in death her deceased lord, whether (if low caste) buried alive with his corpse or (if high caste) consumed alive with him on his funeral pyre, so that, as one together in death, the two should be brought as one to eternal life: the wife becoming thus the sacramental counterpart of Christ Crucified in the Christian image, as Savior unto eternity of her spouse in the house of death.

And the celestial sign of the efficacy of such "death following" was recognized, both in India and throughout the Near East, in the celestial exemplar of the planet Venus, first as Evening, then as Morning Star: first, following her lord, the Sun, into night and then leading him forth to renewed day. As Venus, Ishtar, Satī, Isis, Inanna, and the rest, that is to say, the Goddess of Many Names, of the ancients, functioned and was revered universally as the source and being, not only of all temporal life, but also of life eternal. In Sumer, as Ninhursag, we see her in the first role and, as Inanna, in the second, while in daily life she was to be perceived in every woman. For as expressed by the nineteenth-century Hindu saint Ramakrishna, "All women (according to this way of thought) are the embodiments of Sakti. It is Primal Power that has become women and appears in the form of women."[19]

MĀYĀ-ŚAKTI-DEVĪ

The earliest and richest aggregate of testimonials to the character and functionality of this all-embracing and supporting, universal divinity in the earliest period and theater of her preeminency is that illustrated and expounded in Marija Gimbutas's unprecedented exposition. And the fundamental original trait of the Goddess there represented at the opening of her historic career is that she was at that time bisexual, absolute, and single in her generative role. "As a supreme Creator who creates from her own substance, she is the primary goddess," Gimbutas declares, "of the Old European pantheon. In this she contrasts with the Indo-European Earth Mother, who is the impalpable sacred earth-spirit and is not in herself a creative principle; only through the interaction of the sky-god does she become pregnant."[20]

The idea is equivalent to that which in India is implicit in the compound noun *māyā-śakti-devī*, the "goddess" (*devī*), as at once the "moving energy" (*śakti*) and the "illusion" (*māyā*) of phenomenality. For according to this nondualistic type of cosmogonic metaphor, the universe as *māyā* is *brahman*, the Imperishable, as perceived. It is thus its own sole cause as well as substance. The analogy is given in the *Muṇḍaka Upanishad* of a spider and its web.

"As the spider brings forth and takes back its thread . . . so creation springs from the Imperishable."[21] And further, in the *Vedāntasāra*: "As from its own standpoint the spider is the efficient cause of its web, from the point of view of its body it is also its material cause."[22]

In distinct contrast to the Creation attributed some six millennia later to the male Creator God, who in Gen. 1:27 is represented (like the Neolithic World Mother) as bisexual yet in Gen. 2:7 is declared to have

> formed man of dust from the ground and breathed into his nostrils the breath of life, the creation and creatures of the all-creating Goddess are of her own substance. The dust itself is of her body; not inert but alive. Nor was there, at any time, an unformed "chaos" to which form had to be given by a god's intention. Form, in this nondual view, is of the essence of the cosmogonic process throughout space, which is of her body, and through time, which is equally of her nature.

An outstanding characteristic of many of the artworks illustrated in Gimbutas's volume is the abstract formality of their symbolically adorned and proportioned forms. In Gimbutas's words,

> While the Cycladic figurines of the third millennium B.C. are the most extremely geometricised, rigid constraint of this kind, though less marked, characterizes most of the groups of Old European Neolithic and Chalcolithic figures. . . . Supernatural powers were conceived as an explanatory device to induce an ordered experience of nature's irregularities. These powers were given form as masks, hybrid figures and animals, producing a symbolic, conceptual art not given to physical naturalism.[23]

Painted or inscribed upon these symbolically composed little revelations of powers intuited as informing and moving the whole spectacle of nature were a number of characteristic conventionalized signs or ideograms, which, as recognized by Gimbutas, were of

> two basic categories: those related to water and rain, the snake and the bird; and those associated with the moon, the vegetal life

cycle, the rotation of seasons, the birth and growth essential to the perpetuation of life. The first category consists of symbols with simple parallel lines, V's, zigzags, chevrons and meanders, and spirals. The second group includes the cross, the encircled cross and more complex derivations of this basic motif which symbolically connects the four corners of the world, the crescent, horn, caterpillar, egg and fish.[24]

Statuettes of the Goddess in many forms (we have no knowledge of her names at that time) identify her with every one of these tokens of the structuring force of a universe of which she (like the spider at the center of its structured web) is at once the source and the substance. As summarized in Gimbutas's words:

> Female snake, bird, egg, and fish played parts in creation myths, and the female goddess was the creative principle. The Snake Goddess and Bird Goddess create the world, charge it with energy, and nourish the earth and its creatures with the life-giving element conceived as water. The waters of heaven and earth are under their control. The Great Goddess emerges miraculously out of death, out of the sacrificial bull, and in her body the new life begins.[25]

> Compare the New Jerusalem, 4 × 432 billion cubic stadia in volume, like a radiant jewel coming down from God following the sacrifice of the Savior; the Eddic "earth anew from the waves again," following the immolation of 432,000 gods; or the periodic renewals, following the terrible dissolutions every 4,320,000 years, of the Indian Mahāyuga; likewise, the glorious *anodos* of the Virgin, Koré, of the Greek mysteries, following the *kathodos* of her sorrowful descent into the netherworld, in the very way of Inanna, Ishtar, and celestial Venus, first as Evening, then as Morning Star. Compare, also, the predictable reappearances of the vanished moon every 29 days, 12 hours, 44 minutes and 2.8 seconds, following 3 nights of absence from a starlit sky.

THE PULSE OF BEING

At what period and in what part of the archaic world did the number 432,000 become attached to the system of signs symbolic of the predictable renewals after periodic dissolutions of a living universe which in the iconography of Old Europe had been imaged as the body of its Creator? The datings recognized by Gimbutas for the relevant regions of the Old European Neolithic are as follows:[26]

I. *The Aegean and Central Balkan Area*
Neolithic, ca. 7000–5500 B.C.
Chalcolithic, ca. 5500–3500 B.C.

II. *The Adriatic Area*
Neolithic, ca. 7000–5500 B.C.
Advanced Neolithic-Chalcolithic, ca. 5500–3500 B.C.

III. *The Middle Danube Basin*
Neolithic, ca. 5500–4500 B.C.
Advanced Neolithic and Chalcolithic, ca. 5000–3500 B.C.

IV. *The East Balkan Area*
Neolithic, ca. 6500–5000 B.C.
Chalcolithic, ca. 5000–3500 B.C.

V. *The Moldavian-West Ukranian Area*
Neolithic, ca. 6500–5000 B.C.
Chalcolithic, ca. 5000–3500 B.C.

7000–3500 B.C. are then the bounding dates of this epoch in the chronology of the evolution of consciousness in Old Europe. Engraved signs which have been interpreted as giving evidence of a "linear Old European script" have been identified on as many as one out of every hundred of the Chalcolithic statuettes, as well as upon numerous plaques, dishes, spindle-whorls, and other objects devoted, from ca. 5500 B.C., as votive offerings to the Goddess.[27] No signs have yet been reported, however, of a knowledge at that time of any such order of mathematical symbolics as the recognition of cycles of 43,200 or 432,000 years would have required.

The earliest recognizable mathematical documents known to archaeology are from Sumer, third millennium B.C., and their system of numeration is sexagesimal (base 60). As interpreted by Kramer:

> The mathematical school texts which have come down to us are of two types: tables and problems. The former include tabulations of reciprocals, multiplications, squares and square roots,

cubes and cube roots, the sums of squares and cubes needed for the numerical solution of certain types of equations, exponential functions, coefficients giving numbers for practical computation (like the approximate value of the square root of 2), and numerous metrological calculations giving areas of rectangles, circles, etc. The problem texts deal with Pythagorean numbers, cubic roots, equations, and such practical matters as excavating or enlarging canals, counting bricks, and so on. As of today, almost all problem texts are Akkadian, although they must go back in large part to Sumerian prototypes since nearly all the technical terms used are Sumerian.[28]

Indeed, a Sumerian tablet of about 2500 B.C. from the ruins of Shuruppak, home city of the Flood hero Ziusudra, already contains a table for the calculation in sexagesimal terms of the surfaces of square-shaped fields.[29]

In what period this method of mathematical calculation was first applied to measurement of the movements of the celestial lights, no one has yet determined. However, as a moment's attention to a calculator will demonstrate, $60 \times 60 \times 60 \times 2 = 432,000$, while $60 \times 60 \times 60 \times 60 \times 2 = 25,920,000$; 25,920 being the number of years required in the precession of the equinoxes for the completion of one full circuit of the Zodiac, since, as already remarked in discussion of Julius Oppert's observations touching the relevance of the biblical sum of 1656 years to Berossos's 432,000, the advance of the equinoctial points along the Zodiacal celestial way proceeds at the rate of 1 degree in 72 years. And 360 degrees $\times$ 72 years $= 25,920$ years, for one completion of a Zodiacal round, which period has for centuries been known as a Great or Platonic Year. But 25,920 divided by 60 equals 432. And so again this number appears, now, however, in exact relation to a scientifically verifiable cosmological eon or cycle of time.

Moreover, as I learned some years ago from a popular handbook on physical fitness,[30] a man in perfect condition, at rest, has normally a heart rate of approximately 1 beat per second: 60 beats a minute; 3,600 beats an hour; in 12 hours 43,200 beats and in 24 hours 86,400. So we hold this measure in our hearts, as well as in the manufactured watches on our wrists. Can it be that the Old

Sumerians, ca. 2500 B.C., might already have had some notion of the relevance of their sexagesimal system to the mathematics of any such macro-micro-meso-cosmic coordination?

From an authoritative work on Indian tantra yoga I learn that, according to the *Dhyānabindu* and other related Upanishads, all living beings inhale and exhale 21,600 times a day,[31] this being in evidence of their spiritual as well as physical identity in the nature of the universal *māyā-śakti-devī,* the Great Goddess who in India is celebrated in a litany of her 108 names. $21,600 \times 2 = 43,200$. But $108 \times 2 = 216$, while $108 \times 4 = 432$, and $432 \times 60 = 25,920$.

It was H. V. Hilprecht in Philadelphia at the University Museum in 1905, poring over literally thousands of cuneiform clay fragments upon which mathematical reckonings were inscribed, who first recognized this last figure, which is of the Great or Platonic Year, among remains of such early date. In his report, published 1906, he wrote, "All the multiplication and division tables from the temple libraries of Nippur and Sippar and from the library of Ashurbanipal are based upon 12,960,000." And as he there pointed out, $12,960 \times 2 = 25,920$.[32] Alfred Jeremias was inclined to accept this discovery as indicating the likelihood of a recognition of the precession in Mesopotamia as early as the third or perhaps even fourth millennium B.C. "If this interpretation is correct and the figure really does refer to the precession," he wrote, "then it proves that before Hipparchus an exact reckoning of the precession had been achieved, which later was forgotten."[33] And he wrote again, "It is, in fact, incredible that the Babylonians, experienced as they were in the observation of the heavens, should not have deduced from the difference between earlier and later observations a shift of the equinoctial point. . . . As soon as the position of the sun at the time of the spring equinox became a point of observation, the precession during centuries *must* have been noticed. . . . Indeed in the course of one year it comes to 50 seconds, and during longer periods cannot possibly have been ignored."[34]

It is generally held that an Asiatic Greek, Hipparchus of Bithynia (fl. 146–128 B.C.), in a treatise entitled, "On the Displacement of the Solstitial and Equinoctial Signs," was the first to have recognized the precession of the equinoxes and that it was then not until A.D. 1526 that the exact reading was announced of 1 degree every 72 years. Yet the Chaldean priest Berossos, a century and a half before Hipparchus's time, had already taken seriously the number 432,000, as had, also at that time, the compilers of Genesis 5–7, whose antediluvian cycle of exactly 1,656 years shared as factor with Berossos the critical precessional term 72. The still earlier possibility suggested by Hilprecht and Jeremias of a Sumerian anticipation of all this in the third or fourth millennium B.C. has not, as far as I know, been further examined or even seriously discussed.

So that, although it is reasonably certain that it was in Sumer, ca. 3500–2500 B.C., that the figure 25,920 divided by 60 equals 432 first became associated with the order of a universe, which in the Neolithic period had been revered as the body of a goddess, we know little or nothing of the stages and processes by which these two distinct traditions—the earlier of mythology, folklore, mysticism, and legend; the later of mathematical logic, cosmological inquiry, rational and speculative thought—were brought together and conjoined. All that can be confidently said is that by the sixth century B.C. at the very latest, in the mathematically formulated speculations of the mystical, secretive brotherhood founded by the Samian sage Pythagoras (born on the island of Samos in the Aegean, ca. 580 B.C.; died in Metapontum, Italy, ca. 500 B.C.)—whose fundamental dictum, "all is number," had opened the way to a systematic study of the mathematics of form and harmony which united, as of one transcendent science epitomized in music, the laws at once of outer space (cosmology), inner space (psychology), and the arts (aesthetics)—the two, apparently contrary approaches of the visionary and the empiricist were brought and held together as substantially in accord.

Reconstruction of the scientistic *mythos* of Pythagoras has been rendered for scholars problematic by the fact that the master himself (like the Buddha, his oriental contemporary, ca. 563–483 B.C.) left no writings. Furthermore, the mystical brotherhood that he founded in southern Italy not only was governed by rules of secrecy but in the middle of the fifth century B.C. was forcibly disbanded and its membership dispersed. Sources purporting to represent the movement go back at best to fourth-century sources, which are already uncritical in character and often amalgams of Pythagorean, Orphic, and Neo-Platonic information.[35] Hence, it is impossible to determine how much of what has come down to us can be attributed to Pythagoras himself, how much may have been derived by him from the general body of mystic lore already shared by the numerous gurus of his day throughout the Near, Middle, and Far East, or how much of this esoteric learning may have become assimilated to the movement centuries later.

The idea, for example, of sound (Sanskrit *śabda*) as generator of the perceived universe is fundamental to the Vedas and all later Hindu thought. Alain Daniélou, in his *Introduction to the Study of Musical Scales,* quotes from a commentary on a Sivaite Sutra:

> The initiating point (*bindu*), desirous to manifest the thought which it holds of all things, vibrates, transformed into a primordial sound of the nature of a cry (*nāda*). *It shouts out the universe, which is not distinct from itself.* That is to say, it thinks it. Hence the term, *śabda,* "word." Meditation is the supreme "word": it "sounds," that is to say, "vibrates," submitting all things to the fragmentation of life. This is how it is *nāda,* "vibration." This is what is meant by the saying: "Sound (*śabda*), which is of the nature of *nāda,* resides in all living beings."[36]

Likewise, in the Chinese "Book of Rites," *Li Chi,* which, as Daniélou reminds us, was edited by Confucius (ca. 551–478 B.C., again a contemporary of Pythagoras), we are told,

> Music makes for common union. Rites make for difference and distinction. From common union comes mutual affection; from difference, mutual respect. . . . Music comes from within; rites act from without. Coming from within, music produces serenity of mind. Acting from without, rites produce the finished elegance of manner. Great music must be easy. Great rites must be simple. Let music achieve its full results, and there will be no resentments. Let rites achieve their full results, and there will be no contentions. The reason why bowings and courtesies could set the world in order is that there are music and rites.[37]

Tung Chung-shu, a later Confucian scholar, second century B.C., expanded upon these thoughts:

> Tuned to the tone of Heaven and Earth," he wrote, "the vital spirits of man express all the tremors of Heaven and Earth, exactly as several citharas, all tuned on *Kung* (the tonic), all vibrate when the note *Kung* resounds. The fact of the harmony between Heaven and Earth and Man does not come from a physical union, from a direct action, it comes from a tuning on the same note producing vibrations in unison. . . . In the Universe there is no hazard, there is no spontaneity; all is influence and harmony, accord answering accord.[38]

A characteristic Pythagorean symbolic diagram cited by all authorities as in some way epigrammatical of an essential doctrine of the movement is the so-called *tetraktys,* or "triangle of fourness," which can be viewed either as an equilateral triangle of 9 points composed around a single central point or as a pyramid of 10 points arranged in 3 expanding stages of descent, respectively of 2, 3, and 4 (= 9) points, unfurling from a single point at the summit. The Pythagoreans, by all accounts, regarded even numbers (2, 4, 6, and so on) as female; uneven (3, 5, 7, and so on), as male; interpreting 1 as neither even nor odd but germinal of both series, corresponding thus to the Indian tantric *bindu,* "desirous to manifest the thought which it holds of all things." As *nāda,* vibrating, transformed into primordial sound, this initiating impulse "shouts out the universe, which is not distinct from itself"; that creative "shout" being in modern terms the Big Bang of creation, whence from a single point of inconceivable intensity this entire expanding universe exploded, flying into distances that are still receding.

In Indian mystical utterance this universal Sound is announced as OM. In oriental model music it is represented in the tonic in relation to which the melody is heard. And in Pythagorean thought it was identified with *Proslambanomene,* the supporting ground tone, A, which thereby was considered to have 432 vibrations (whereas the pitch in modern tunings is raised to around

440). Musically, as Daniélou points out, the primal sound given measure yields first its octave (2/1), after which a third tone, the fifth (3/2), is heard, in relation to which the others then find place.[39] And in this regard he cites a verse from the *Tao Te Ching:* "The Tao produced One; One produced Two; Two produced Three; Three produced all things."[40]

In Indian thought the first characteristic of *māyā* (from the verbal root *mā,* "to measure") is duality; and for the Pythagoreans, likewise, the world-process was a complex of dualities sprung from the imposition of "limitation" or "measure" (= *māyā*) upon the "unlimited" (*brahman*); the "unlimited" and its "limitation" then being the first of a series of nine further pairs of opposites: odd and even, light and dark, and so on, essentially the Chinese *yang* and *yin.*

Out of the stress of such a context of universal polarization, the Indian (Sānkhya) philosophers recognized as arising three "qualities or characteristics" (*guṇas*), through the interrelation of which all of "nature" (*prakṛiti*) was seen as motivated; namely, "inertia, mass, or heaviness" (*tamas*); "energy and vitality" (*rajas*); and the "harmony or clarity" (*sattva*) of any balanced relationship of the opposed two. In Pythagorean terms, the same three would correspond, respectively, to (1) the "unlimited," (2) the "limiting," and (3) the "harmony" or "fitting together" (*harmonia*) of any "beautiful order of things" (*kosmos*), whether as a macrocosm (the universe), microcosm (an individual), or mesocosm (ideal society or work of art). And the number representative in that system of such a visible order is 4.

And so now, counting the number of points of the Pythagorean *tetraktys,* from the base upward to the creative *bindu* (beyond number) at the top, the sum of their sequence, 4–3–2, is of course 9; as is that, also, of 2–1–6 (which is half of 432); as well as of 1–0–8 (half of 216); which last is the number of her names recited in worship of the Indian Great Goddess, Kālī, Durgā, Umā, Sitā, Satī (pronounced Suttee), and Pārvatī ("Daughter of the Mountain"). Moreover, the total 9 is implicit, also, in the sum of years of the biblical 10 patriarchs, from the day of Adam's creation to that of the end of the antediluvian age in Noah's Flood, since $1 + 6 + 5 + 6 = 18$, while $1 + 8 = 9$. And finally, most remarkably, in the course of the precession of the equinoxes the number of years required for the completion of one circuit of the Zodiac at the rate of 1 degree in 72 years (noting that $7 + 2 = 9$), is $2 + 5 + 9 + 2 + 0 = 18$, where again, $1 + 8 = 9$.

CREATRESS AND REDEMPTRESS

"Nine times now, since my birth," wrote Dante at the opening of his early book of poems, *La Vita Nuova*,

the heaven of light had turned almost to the same point in its own gyration, when the glorious Lady of my mind, who was called Beatrice by many who knew not what to call her, first appeared before my eyes. She had already been in this life so long that in its course the starry heaven had moved toward the region of the East one of the twelve parts of a degree; so that at the beginning of her ninth year she appeared to me, and I near the end of my ninth year saw her. She appeared to me clothed in a most noble color, a modest and becoming crimson, and she was girt and adorned in such wise as befitted her very youthful age. At that instant, I say truly that the spirit of life, which dwells in the most secret chamber of the heart, began to tremble with such violence that it appeared fearfully in the least pulses, and, trembling, said these words: *Ecce deus fortior me, qui veniens dominabitur mihi* [Behold a god stronger than I, who coming shall rule over me]. . . .

And further:

When so many days had passed that nine years were exactly complete since the above described apparition of this most gentle lady, on the last of these days it happened that this admirable lady appeared to me, clothed in purest white, between two gentle ladies who were of greater age; and, passing along a street, turned her eyes toward that place where I stood very timidly; and by her ineffable courtesy, which is today rewarded in the eternal world, saluted me with such virtue that it seemed to me then that I saw all the bounds of bliss. The hour when her most sweet salutation reached me was precisely the ninth of that day. . . .

At the age of twenty-four, June 8, 1290, Beatrice Portinare died, and the whole universe for Dante became so filled thereafter with the radiance of her angelic grace that in thought of her alone his heart was lifted to her place in heaven, in the sight of God. Writing of the mystery of the cosmic measure of her glory he wrote

> I say that, according to the mode of reckoning in Arabia, her most noble soul departed in the first hour of the ninth day of the month; and, according to the reckoning in Syria, she departed in the ninth month of the year, since the first month there is Tisrin, which with us is October. And according to our reckoning, she departed in that year of our indiction, that is, of the years of the Lord, in which the perfect number was completed for the ninth time in that century in which she had been set in this world; and she was of the Christians of the thirteenth century.
>
> One reason why this number was so friendly to her may be this: since, according to Ptolemy and according to the Christian truth, there are nine heavens which move, and, according to the common astrological opinion, the said heavens work effects here below according to their respective positions, this number was her friend to the end that it might be understood that at her generation all the nine movable heavens were in most perfect relation. This is one reason thereof; but considering more subtlely and according to the infallible truth, this number was she herself; I mean by similitude, and I intend it thus: the number three is the root of nine, for without any other number, multiplied by itself it makes nine, as we see plainly that three times three make nine. Therefore, since three is the factor by itself of nine, and the Author of miracles by himself is three, namely, Father, Son, and Holy Spirit, who are three and one, this lady was accompanied by the number nine, that it might be understood that she was a nine, that is, a miracle, whose only root is the marvellous Trinity. . . .[41]

The Pythagorean *tetraktys,* viewed as an upward-pointing triangle built of 9 points with a tenth, as *bindu,* in the center, suggests an Indian tantric diagram (*yantra*) symbolic of the female power in its spiritually alluring role recognized by Goethe in the last two lines of his *Faust: Das Ewig-Weibliche/Zieht uns hinan!*

Gimbutas, writing of the geometric diagrams engraved on the statuettes of Old Europe, ca. 7000–3500 B.C., gives special attention to the lozenge with a dot in the center. "The dot, representing seed, and the lozenge, symbolizing the sown field," she writes, "appear on sculptures of an enthroned pregnant goddess and are also incised or painted on totally schematized figurines. . . . A lozenge is often the most prominent feature, the rest of the female body serving only as a background to the ideographic concept."[42]

Among the best known of those Indian tantric diagrams known as *yantras,* designed to inspire and support meditation, that of the *downward* pointing triangle with a dot in its center is an explicit symbol of female energy in its generative role. This triangle is an adaptation of the prominent genital triangle of the typical Neolithic female statuette. The dot is known as the *bindu,* the "drop" (which, like a drop of oil in water, expands), and the triangle as the *yoni* (womb, vagina, vulva; place of origin, birth, and rest). As contemplated by the Sakti worshiper, the whole sign is of the Goddess, alone, as *māyā-śakti-devī,* in the sense of those earliest Neolithic figurines, recognized and interpreted by Gimbutas, of the Goddess "absolute and single in her generative role," at once the cause and the substance (like the spider in its web) of this living universe and its life.

In those yantras where the dot or "drop" is unfolded, however, it is represented in India as a phallos, a *lingam;* so that, whereas in the dot/triangle symbol the connotation might have been appropriately read either as of the Goddess alone or as of a goddess and a god in union, here, although the "seed" and the "field" are still together *within* the Goddess, the image is now explicitly of the male and female organs joined. The earlier, nondualistic image has been turned, that is to say, into a dualistic symbol, transferring from the female to the male the initiating moment and impulse of creation.

This radically distinct construction must represent and have closely followed upon the critical historic turn, dated by Gimbutas to ca. 3500 B.C., from the earlier Neolithic and Chalcolithic concept of the Goddess as sole cause and very substance of the body of this universe to an Indo-European or Semitic, dualistic manner of symbolization, where she is no longer in herself and alone "Great" but the consort of a "Great" God.

There is in Hesiod's *Theogony* an unmistakable hint of this change, where Gaia, the Earth, is represented as the mother of the heaven-god, her spouse.

"First of all there came Chaos and after him," we read, "came Gaia of the broad breast, to be the unshakable foundation of all the immortals. . . . But Gaia's first born was one who matched her in every dimension, Ouranos, the starry sky, to cover her all over. . . . She lay with Ouranos and bore him deep-swirling Okeanos. . . ."[43]

Likewise in the Old Testament, Proverbs 8, the Great Goddess in her character as "Wisdom" reveals herself as having been from the beginning with Yahweh as cocreator.

> The Lord created me [Hebrew, *ganani,* in other versions trans-
> lated as "possessed me" or "acquired me"][44] at the beginning of
> his work, the first of his acts of old. Ages ago, I was set up, at the
> first, before the beginning of the earth. When there were no
> depths I was brought forth, when there were no springs abound-
> ing with water. Before the mountains had been shaped, before
> the hills, I was brought forth; before he had made the earth with
> its fields, or the first of the dust of the world. When he estab-
> lished the heavens, I was there, when he drew a circle on the face
> of the deep, when he made firm the skies above, when he
> established the foundations of the deep, when he assigned to the
> sea its limit, so that the waters might not transgress his com-
> mand, when he marked out the foundations of the earth, then I
> was beside him, like a master workman; and I was daily his
> delight, rejoicing before him always, rejoicing in his inhabited
> world and delighting in the sons of men.
>
> And now, my sons, listen to me: happy are those who keep
> my ways. . . . (Prov. 8:22–32)

The *upward* pointing triangle, both of the Indian *yantras* and of the Pythagorean *tetraktys,* like its downward pointing counterpart, is susceptible of two readings, whether as of the Goddess alone or as of the Goddess in union with a male of her own birth, who may even (as in both the Bible and the Koran) finally usurp her role and character as sole creator—not of a universe identical with himself, however, but of a cosmological artifact, distinct from and subordinate to his unique, unnatural, and finally irrelevant divinity.

There is from India an astonishing tantric image known as *cinna masta* (pronounced chinna masta, of the "severed head"), which is of the Goddess cutting off her own head to release her devotees or children from the bondage of her māyā. The Greek figure of beheaded Medusa, from the stump of whose neck the winged steed Pegasus flies to become a constellation, is a counterpart of this symbolic form. In later classical times, the winged steed in soaring flight was interpreted as allegorical of the soul released from the body to immortality, and by the masters of the Renaissance the same ascending flight was read as of poetic inspiration—which cannot come to birth until the obstacle of the rationalizing head is removed.

In medieval Christian thought, the two contrary forces symbolized in the downward and upward pointing triangles were personified, respectively, in Eve and the Virgin Mary, through the second of whom the effects of her predecessor's Original Sin were reversed. The idea is aptly rendered in the Latin pun of a popular Catholic hymn still sung to the Virgin as "Star of the Sea," *Ave Maris Stella,* where the upward turn is suggested simply by reversing Eva's name to Ave:

Ave maris stella,	Hail, O Star of ocean,
Dei Mater alma,	God's own Mother blest,
Atque semper Virgo,	Ever sinless Virgin,
Felix coeli porta.	Gate of heav'nly rest.
Sumens illud Ave	Taking that sweet Ave
Gabrielis ore,	Which from Gabriel came,
Funda nos in pace,	Peace confirm within us,
Mutans hevae nomen.	Changing Eva's name.[45]

THE MUSES NINE

In the "year of our Lord" 1439, an ecumenical council of the Roman Catholic church which had been assembled in Ferrara to attempt to resolve the delicate *filioque* argument, that in 1054 had separated the Greek and Latin churches, was transferred to Cosimo de' Medici's Florence when a plague hit the earlier city. A large and distinguished Greek delegation was in attendance, and the Medici was so inspired with admiration for their Platonic, Neoplatonic, and Pythagorean learning that he determined forthwith to establish on his own estate at Careggi an academy on the model of Plato's in Athens (which in A.D. 529, along with all the other pagan institutions of that time, had been closed by order of the Emperor Justinian).

With the fall of Constantinople in 1453 to the Turks and the subsequent appearances in the Latin West of Greek manuscripts from Byzantium brought by refugee priests and monks, the historic moment arrived for Cosimo to begin reassembling in his villa as much as might be ever retrieved of the vestiges of classical learning. The University of Florence —likewise alerted by the council—had in 1439 resumed the teaching of the Greek language, which, except in the monasteries and abbeys of Ireland, had been lost to the Latin West for more than seven hundred years. The young Marsilio Ficino (1433–99), an ardent student of both Greek and Latin, had become the Medici's chief translator and advisor, and with the willing cooperation of the victorious sultan Mehmed II himself, Cosimo initiated and organized a thoroughgoing, systematic search for manuscripts that in good time yielded the founding core of an incomparable library, which was later named, after Cosimo's grandson, the Lorentian (Laurenziana).

In this way, through the enterprise of a single inspired individual, the vast catastrophe to the intelligence of Europe which had followed upon the deliberate destruction in A.D. 391 of the irreplaceable Alexandrian library, research center, and museum (Greek, *Mouseion,* from *Mouseios,* "of the Muses") was in some measure redressed. Reputed to have contained no less than 500,000 volumes burned to extinction by Christian zealots, the *Mouseion* had been a center, not only of Hellenistic, Neoplatonic, and Pythagorean learning, but also of Semitic. The Septuagint translation into Greek of the Old Testament had been made there. And that there were influences from India as well cannot be doubted, since already as early as the fourth century B.C. the Buddhist emperor Asoka (as reported in his rock-carved edicts) had sent teachers of the Buddhist Dharma, not only to the court of Ptolemy II of Egypt (the Ptolemies were the founders of the *Mouseion*), but also to Antiochus II of Syria, Magas of Cyrene, Antigonas Gonatus of Macedonia, and Alexander II of Epirus.[46] Plotinus, the founder of Neoplatonism, born A.D. 205 in Egypt, commenced his career in Alexandria. Theon, the fourth century mathematician to whose recension of Euclid's *Elements* we owe our knowledge of that work, was also a contributor to the dignity of that culminating Hellenistic center of universal learning. His extraordinary daughter Hypatia, the first notable woman in mathematics and the recognized head of the Alexandrian Neoplatonist school of her day, born A.D. 370, was in March 415 mob-murdered by a mass of monks and general Christian fanatics spiritually inflamed by contagion of their recently installed, vigorously antipagan bishop, now canonized, St. Cyril of Alexandria. Whereafter, submerged beneath an increasing tide of "barbarism and religion" (to use Edward Gibbon's phrase), magnificent Alexandria sank to historical insignificance, only the flotsam and jetsam of its invaluable treasury to be ever retrieved.

However, the galaxy of inspired artists—sculptors, architects, and painters—who appeared as by magic around the philosophical oasis of Cosimo's reconstituted academy and library was amazing. And that his harvest of antiquity, translated from Greek into Latin largely by Marsilio Ficino, had indeed revived the inspiration of late classic spirituality is evident in every detail of the works of art of that moment of Europe's reawakening to its native heritage. It was as though the Muses had themselves awakened and found voice. For among the sculptors of that company were Donatello and Ghiberti; among the architects, Brunelleschi and Michelozzo;

painters, Fra Angelico, Andrea del Castagno, and Benozzo Gozzoli; while of the second generation—of the period of Cosimo's grandson Lorenzo the Magnificent (1449–92), whose teacher had been Ficino—we read of Verrocchio and his pupils Leonardo da Vinci, Botticelli, and Michelangelo; the last named having begun his career at the age of fifteen as a pupil in the sculpture school in Lorenzo's garden.

Pico della Mirandola (1463–94) was another inspired associate of this incredible academy, who, having studied not only Latin and Greek but Arabic, Hebrew, and Aramaic as well, was the first Christian philosopher to apply Cabbalistic learning to the support of Christian theological propositions. In 1486, he arranged for a pan-European assemblage in Rome before which he would announce and defend nine hundred theses drawn from Latin, Greek, Hebrew, and Arabic sources. Thirteen of his theses were declared heretical, however, and the assembly was forbidden by the pope.

Yet the depth and range of his learning, reaching back to those centuries of syncretic, transcultural philosophical formulations which had followed upon Alexander the Great's "marriage of East and West" (out of which, indeed, the dogmas of the Latin church had themselves evolved), survived the papal ban. For his bold comparative insights, interpreting Egyptian, Hebrew, Greek, and Christian mythic and symbolic forms as culturally distinguished metaphors of a single, universally consistent *poetica theologica,* perfectly represented the expanding spirit and world horizon through which Renaissance art and thought were being released in his day from the inbred, tight little fold of the Middle Ages. At the Medici Villa di Careggi, sculpture, architecture, painting, and philosophy were of one accord in the representation of *all* names and forms, whether of the mind or of the world beheld, as equally radiant of some universal mystery.

In the allegorical diagram of the "Music of the Spheres" that was published in 1496 as the frontispiece of Francinus Gafurius's *Practica musice,* this idea of a mystery partly revealed is suggested by the clothing of the Muses, whose forms appear in descending series at the left of the composition.

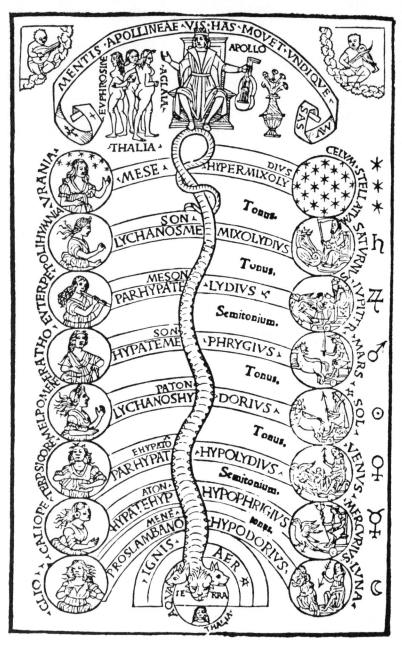

FIG. 2. The Music of the Spheres. From Francinus Gafurius, *Practica Musice* (Florence, 1496).

Their number, like that which Dante associated with Beatrice, is 9; for their root, too, is a trinity. However, the trinity here is not of three male divinities with the Virgin then as a feminine fourth but of the classical three Graces with Apollo as a masculine fourth. And as the Muses are here clothed, so the Graces, performing their round-dance on the noumenal plane beyond and above the visible sky, directly in the presence of Apollo, are unclothed. They are the triune personifications of the Aristotelean *primum mobile,* or "first moving thing," which is of the tenth or highest celestial sphere and derives its circular motion directly from God, the "unmoved mover." Here the image of God, as Apollo, is clothed, since the "unmoved being" of such a "first cause" transcends envisionment (i.e., all names and forms); whereas the Graces are movement itself. As stated in the Latin of the inscribed scroll overhead: "The energy or virtue (*vis*) of the Apollonian mind moves or inspires (*movet*) everywhere the Muses."

Both the names and the postures of the Graces tell of the qualities of their influence: (1) Thalia ("Blooming, Abundance"), unites and relates her opposed companions; (2) Euphrosyne ("Mirth, Festivity, Good Cheer"), moves away from the God to the descent, ninefold, of the Muses; while (3) Aglaia ("Splendor, Beauty, Triumph, Adornment"), confronts him, returning to source.

Pico and Ficino revered these three as an exemplary triad archetypal of all the others of classical myth. In Pico's words, "He that understands profoundly and clearly how the unity of Venus is unfolded in the trinity of the Graces, and the unity of Necessity in the trinity of the Fates, and the unity of Saturn in the trinity of Jupiter, Neptune, and Pluto, knows the proper way of proceeding in Orphic theology."[47] For as Edgar Wind points out in comment on this passage, "it was an axiom of Platonic theology that every god exerts his power in a triadic rhythm."[48]

"The bounty bestowed by the gods upon lower beings," states Wind, continuing, "was conceived by the Neoplatonists as a kind of overflowing (*emanatio*), which produced a vivifying rapture or conversion (called by Ficino *conversio, rapto,* or *vivificatio*) whereby the lower beings were drawn back to heaven and rejoined the gods (*remeatio*)." Moreover: "The munificence of the gods having thus been unfolded in the triple rhythm of *emanatio, rapto,* and *remeatio,* it was possible to recognize in this sequence the divine model of what Seneca had defined as the circle of grace: giving, accepting, and returning. . . . But in Proclus, *Elements of Theology,* prop. 35 (Dodds, 1933, pp. 38f), the sequence reads: (1) inheritence in the cause, (2) procession from the cause, (3) reversion to the cause; and that is the original Neoplatonic scheme."[49]

Translated into Christian trinitarian terms, this triadic revelation of divine grace would appear as (1) the Father, (2) the Son, and (3) the Holy Spirit, three hypostases or "persons" in one godhead, with the idea of the "godhead" represented in Gafurius's design by the clothed Apollo and that of the "persons" or hypostases by the Graces, who in Indian tantric terms are exactly *māyā-śakti-devī,* or in the Sāṅkhya view (as noticed above), *prakṛiti,* of three *guṇas* or "characteristics," *sattva, rajas,* and *tamas.*

The serpentine, triple-headed form flowing down the center of the composition is Gafurius's adaptation to his design of a symbolic figure that in Alexandria had been associated with an image of the composite Egypto-Greco-Roman God Serapis. "In the great temple of Serapis at Alexandria," states Wind, from whose *Pagan Mysteries in the Renaissance* I have reproduced this chart,

> the image of the Egypto-Hellenic god was attended by a triple-headed Monster resembling Cerberus [the watchdog at the gate to Hades] but with this difference that the three heads of the [Alexandrian] beast were distinguished as wolf, lion, and dog. The most informative ancient text on this attribute . . . is Macrobius, *Saturnalia* I, xx, where the three heads are explained as signifying the three parts of Time: facing left, the voracious wolf represents the vanished past; the hopefully sniffing dog looks to the right, anticipating the future; while the present, in the middle, is embodied in the majestic lion seen full-face. Petrarch's *Africa* III, 162ff., gives a splendid description of the three heads, followed by a concise statement of the allegory: *fugientia tempora signant.*[50]

Dante, it will be recalled, at the opening of *Inferno* I, 28–68, tells of three beasts that in a savage wood confronted him, barring his way to Salvation: a lion, signifying Pride; a leopard, luxurious Desire; and a she-wolf, Violence and Fear. Dante's leopard is equivalent to Gafurius's hopefully sniffing, Alexandrian dog, and the triad of obstructive sentiments named is exactly of those three temptations that were overcome by the Buddha in yoga at the foot of the Bodhi-tree: "desire" (*kāma*), fear of "death" (*māra*), and attachment to temporal social ideals (*dharma*).

There is an immediately evident and more than coincidental likeness of Gafurius's serpent descending through a graded universe to the Indian idea of a yogic "serpent channel" descending from the crown of the head, down the spinal column to a "lotus center" located between the anus and genitalia that is known as "Root Support" (*mūlādhāra*), where the spiritual energy (*śakti*) of the unawakened individual sleeps, coiled on itself like a dormant snake (Sanskrit *kuṇḍalinī*, "coiled serpent"), which is to be aroused through yoga and brought, uncoiling, up the spinal channel to a radiant lotus at the crown of the head called "Thousand Petaled" (*sahasrāra*).

"Gafurius's serpent," Edgar Wind points out,

> is distinguished by a particularly engaging trait. While plunging head-downward into the universe, it curls the end of its tail into a loop on which Apollo ceremoniously sets his feet. A serpent's tail turning back on itself is an image of eternity or perfection (commonly illustrated by a serpent biting its own tail . . .). Gafurius thus makes it diagrammatically clear that Time issues from Eternity, the linear progression of the serpent depends on its attachment to the topmost sphere where its tail coils into a circle."[51]

In Gafurius's design, the circle at the base of the composition, labeled TERRA, corresponds to the yogic "Root Support" where the coiled serpent sleeps. (Serpents shedding their skins to be, as it were, reborn suggest the power of life to cast off death, even to the gaining of eternal life.) The whole upper half of Gafurius's earthly sphere is filled by the vision of those three hovering heads, while below the baseline of the composition, as though hiding below ground, is the first of the nine Muses, whose name, we note, is the same as that of the central member of the unclothed triad of the Graces, namely, Thalia, "Blooming, Abundance." "That the 'descent' of a spiritual force," states Wind, "is compatible with its continuous presence in the 'supercelestial heaven' was a basic tenet of Neoplatonism."

The down-coming of the motivating energy or virtue (*vis*) of the Apollonian mind is here represented as having devolved from the celestial *primum mobile,* represented in the Graces, through their reflexes in the Muses, each of which is shown associated with a planetary sphere, in the pre-Copernican, geocentric, ptolemaic sequence: first, the heaven of fixed stars; next, Saturn, Jupiter, Mars, and the Sun; then, the shadowed spheres of Venus, Mercury, and the Moon; until, finally, wrapped in its increasingly weighty elemental envelopes of Fire (*ignis*), Air (*aer*), and Water (*aqua*), this Earth (*terra*) is entered, where its Muse, unheard, underground, is known as *Surda* ("Silent") *Thalia,* and is a Muse of Nocturnal Silence.

For her voice of the bounty of nature is by her intended poet unheard, whose whole mind is so obsessed by its vision of the hovering monster, *fugientia tempora signant,* that, terrified of his life and of the life also of the world, he has no ear for the gentle whisper of the supportive universe—which is there nevertheless to be heard behind the tricephalous tumult of the beast.

What is therefore required of him, if he is ever to hear that supportive voice, is to forget the passing of time, "regard the lilies of the field . . . and not be anxious" (Matt. 6:28 and 31): place his head, that is to say, together with all its desires and fears for the good of himself and his world directly into the lion's mouth of HERE AND NOW.

In Gen. 3:22–24, we read that when Yahweh drove Adam and Eve from the garden so that they should not "take of the tree of life, and eat, and live forever . . . at the east of the garden of Eden he placed the cherubim, and a flaming sword which turned every way, to guard the way to the tree of life." That sword of flame is the counterpart of the lion's face of Gafurius's monster, while the guarding cherubim correspond to the heads at either side. An essential feature of temple arts generally, whether of Antiquity or of the Orient, is such a threshold feature: two guardians (either in human or in animal form) with a portal between to some sacred precinct.

For example, at Nara (Japan), before the Todaiji Temple with its immense bronze image of "The Great Sun Buddha," Mahavairochana (weight, 452 tons; height, 53 feet, 6 inches; date A.D. 749), there is a large, detached south gate where two imposing giants (26 feet, 6 inches high) stand guard with threatening weapons. The mouth of one is open; that of the other, closed. Fear of death and desire for life would be the immediate sentiments that such an actual pair would excite in any visitor—which are the sentiments to be left behind by anyone passing through, not simply physically as a tourist but for an experience within the sanctuary of release from the pressure of the consciousness of mortality. They correspond to the wolf and leopard of Dante's vision, attending the lion of his pride. So that from this point of view, what is excluding man from the knowledge of his immortality is not the wrath of some external god, but the misadjustment of his own mind. Within the sacred precinct of the Buddhist temple, therefore, seated on a fully opened lotus before the wish-fulfilling "Tree of 'Awakening'" (*bodhi*), the Great Sun Buddha, with his right hand raised in *abhaya-mudrā*, the "fear not posture," and his left extended in the "boon-bestowing posture" *varada-mudrā*, gives freely to all who approach, the gift of his light.

Whereas in contrast (and here is the difference), our biblical Yahweh appears in his unilluminated legend as the archetypal mythic "Hoarder," holding to himself the gift of his grace, and his mythology, consequently, is of man's exile to an earth of dust (Gen. 3:17–19) and of spiritual silence, where no whisper may be heard of Goddess or Muse—except as in that one extraordinary instance, where King Solomon overheard the voice of the Lord God's own Beatrice and Muse, Sophia (Proverbs, *passim,* as above).

No one can possibly function, either as poet or as artist, in any such a desacralized environment. The repudiated and absconded Muse of the living Earth, Surda Thalia, must first be invoked and recalled. And that this may occur, "the cherub with his flaming

sword is hereby commanded," as William Blake has declared in
The Marriage of Heaven and Hell,

> to leave his guard of the tree of life, and when he does, the whole
> creation will be consumed, and appear infinite, and holy, whereas
> it now appears finite and corrupt. This will come to pass by an
> improvement of sensual enjoyment.
>
> But first the notion that man has a body distinct from his
> soul has to be expunged . . . melting apparent surfaces away, and
> displaying the infinite which was hid.
>
> If the doors of perception were cleansed every thing would
> appear to man as it is, infinite. For man has closed himself up, till
> he sees all things thro' the narrow chinks of his cavern.

From the *mūlādhāra,* where the *kuṇḍalinī* sleeps, three portals
open upward, those to right and to left leading to subtle channels
bearing the breaths, respectively, of the left and the right nostrils;
only the portal between opening to the subtle "serpent channel,"
sushumnā ("most gracious, rich in happiness"), leads to the cranial
lotus "Thousand Petalled" (*sahasrāra*), "replete with every form of
bliss, and Pure Knowledge itself."[52]

The channel descending from the left nostril is known as *iḍā*
(nectarous draft, refreshment"); that from the right, as *piṅgalā*
("fiery, tawney red"); the former conducting breath (*prāṇa*) of
"lunar" consciousness, and the latter, of "solar": "solar" consciousness being of eternity, hence threatening to temporal life
(poisonous, fiery, destructive), whereas "lunar" (which is to say,
earthly) is restorative and refreshing. Their two portals in the
mūlādhāra, flanking that of the *sushumnā,* are likened to the guardians at the entrance to a temple and thus correspond in both
position and sense to the wolf and the dog of Gafurius's tricephalous monster.

Now, it can be hardly by coincidence that those overhanging
three heads of Gafurius's Renaissance design, based on ideas
derived from Hellenistic Alexandria, should match in both place-
ment and function the openings upward from the Indian
mūlādhāra. As understood in yogic terms: so long as the two

FIG. 3. Seven Lotus Centers of the Kuṇḍalinī. Drawing by Mark
Hasserlriis.

breaths, left and right, are regarded in a dualistic way as separate
and distinct from each other (as "spirit" and "nature," for example, understood as in opposition), the central portal is closed and
locked. However, the yogi practicing "breath control" (prā-
ṇāyāma), breathing deeply, first in through one nostril, out the

other, then in through the second, out through the first, ensuring each time that the *prāṇa*, the breath, goes all the way down to the *mūlādhāra*, is transforming the opposed breaths into each other as they enter and leave that chamber of the dormant Serpent Power. Untiring, he continues the exercise until, of a sudden, in the *mūlādhāra*, the two breaths blend to a single fire, which like a blast ascends, together with the awakened Serpent, into the suddenly unlocked *sushumnā*.

In Gafurius's design, the symbolized stages of the transformations of consciousness that follow upon the poet's yielding of his head to the lion's mouth (on having muzzled, so to say, the wolf and the dog, or as Blake has described the change of mind, dismissed the cherub with his flaming sword) are represented metaphorically as under inspiration of the Muses graded in relation to the hierarchy of the ptolemaic order of the spheres. Immediately with his recognition of the instant HERE AND NOW, the hidden Muse, *Surda Thalia,* wakes. Her voice is heard. And what until then had been the nocturnal silence of a wasteland of dust and toil becomes eloquent of a universal joy.

For, awake and singing, Thalia, "Blooming and Abundance," is the Muse of bucolic poetry, telling of the innocence and blooming of a living earth. And in this function, her inspiration marks the first stage of the opening of any artist's senses to knowledge of the universal body of which his own is a part. The next Muse of the ascent is Clio (*Kleio,* "Acclaim"), the Muse of history, associated with the earth-shadowed sphere of the Moon; and the following, Calliope (*Kalliope,* "of the Beautiful Voice," once chief and leader of the nine), is of epic poetry and the earth-shadowed sphere of Mercury (= Hermes, guide of souls from the knowledge of time to that of eternity). These first three of the Muses, representing states of mind overshadowed still by concerns of this earth, correspond in the Indian series to the "dispositions of energy" (*śaktis*) of the first three centers of the *sushumnā,* which are namely, *mūlādhāra* (already discussed), *svādhishṭhāna* (spinal center of the region of the genitals), and *maṇipūra* (spinal center of the region of the navel), which are endowed, respectively, with the qualities of the elements earth, water, and fire.

92

The next three Muses together mark the transformation of consciousness that is in yoga associated with the fourth center, *anāhata,* at the level of the heart, and of the element air (breath, *prāṇa, spiritus*). They are (1) Terpsichore, "Joy of the Dance," assigned to the earth-shadowed sphere of Venus; (2) Melpomene, the "Singer," Muse of tragedy and of the fiery sun or "Sun Door" of an opening of the heart to compassion by way of an Aristotelian *katharsis,* or purging of egoity through an access of egoless pity and metaphysical terror; to which (3) Erato, "The Lovely One," attuned to Mars, the first unshadowed sphere, adds lyric poetry.

The Muses of the topmost stages are then of arts suggesting raptures such as yogis at the highest centers of their discipline may know: *viśuddha* ("purified," center of the region of the larynx), *ājñā* ("authority, absolute power": of the inner eye, between the brows), and the *sahasrāra.* The related Muses are Euterpe, "Well Pleasing," Muse of the sphere of Jupiter and dulcet music of the flute; Poly-hymnia, "Sacred Choral Song," of the austere sphere of Saturn; and finally, "The Celestial One," Ourania, of the science of astronomy and sphere of the fixed stars.

On Gafurius's chart, the voices of these sisters, born (as Hesiod tells) of Zeus and "Memory" (*Mnemosyne*), are identified with the ascending tones of the Pythagorean conjoint tetrachord (ABCD EFGA: the A-minor scale), upon which are established the Greek modes: Hypodorian, Hypophrygian, Hypolydian, Dorian, Phrygian, Lydian, Mixolydian, and for good measure, to match the number of the Muses, Hypermixolydian, which is equivalent to Dorian.

The Graces then are pictured above as embodiments of the *primum mobile,* "first moving thing," moved by the energy (*vis*) of the Apollonian mind. However, in what certainly was a much earlier construction, what those Three embodied were aspects of the energy (Sanskrit, *śakti*), not of Apollo, but of the goddess Aphrodite of the fluttering eyelids. Neoplatonically interpreted (as already noticed from Proclus), the three have been allegorized as (1) inheritance in the cause, (2) procession from the cause, and (3) reversion to the cause.[53] Pico and Ficino wrote of them, however, as (1) procession from the cause, (2) rapture by the cause, and (3) return to the cause,[54] in which case the reading is from left to right with the central figure not facing forward, as in Gafurius's design, but with back to the viewer, as in the frequently reproduced Pompeian fresco of the Graces that is now in the Museo Nationale, Naples. Another reading by Ficino of this version of the arrangement was of the triad as allegorical of "Pulcritudo, Amor, and Voluptas," the first issuing from God as a kind of beacon, the second, within the world, moving it to rapture, and the third, returning in a state of joy to its source.[55] There have been, of course, other readings. However, the matter of essential interest here is not of such identifications and allegories, but of the number 3 itself. Aristotle in *De caelo* (1.268a) writes of it as follows:

> The science which has to do with nature clearly concerns itself for the most part with bodies and magnitudes and their properties and movements, but also with the principles of this sort of substance, as many as they may be. For of things constituted by nature some are bodies and magnitudes, some possess body and magnitude, and some are principles of things which possess these. Now a continuum is that which is divisible into parts always capable of subdivision, and a body is that which is every way divisible. A magnitude if divisible one way is a line, if two ways a surface, and if three a body. Beyond these there is no other magnitude, because the three dimensions are all that there are, and that which is divisible in three directions is divisible in all. For, as the Pythagoreans say, the universe and all that is in it is determined by the number three, since beginning and middle and end give the number of the universe, and the number they give is the triad. And so, having taken these three from nature as (so to speak) laws of it, we make further use of the number three in the worship of the Gods.[56]

Plato in *Timaeus* (37d–38b) identifies the number with time, which, as he declares, "imitates eternity and revolves according to a law of number."

"The past and future," he writes,

> are created species of time, which we unconsciously but wrongly transfer to eternal being, for we say that it "was" or "is" or "will be," but the truth is that "is" alone is properly attributed to it,

and that "was" and "will be" are only to be spoken of becoming in time, for they are notions, but that which is immovably the same forever cannot become older or younger by time, nor can it be said that it came into being in the past, or has come into being now, or will come into being in the future, nor is it subject at all to any of those states which affect moving and sensible things and of which generation is the cause. These are the forms of time, which imitates eternity and revolves according to a law of number. Moreover, when we say that what has become *is* become and what becomes *is* becoming, and that what will become *is* about to become and that the nonexistent *is* nonexistent—all these are inaccurate modes of expression.[57]

So that, whether viewed thus by Aristotle as of the nature of things in space or by Plato as of their becoming in time, the number 3 must be recognized as constitutive of phenomenality, which is to say in mythological terms, the body of the Goddess. In Gafurius's design, the number is represented as permeating the universe, from the triad of Graces to the trinity of heads of the monster whose unfolded coil threads the world—which is an idea consistent with the Neoplatonic axiom that in this universe, as a macrocosm, the whole is repeated in every part, as a microcosm.

Wind calls attention to St. Augustine's recognition of an *imago trinitatis in re alia,* as well as of what he interpreted as pagan "vestiges of the trinity" in all the mythologies of his time (supposing the *trinitas* of his own tradition to be, not simply one of many, but the original of all). In the Indian Vedanta, the ultimate triad of names connotative within the field of *māyā* of the universally immanent, metaphysically transcendent *brahmātman* is *sat-cid-ānanda,* namely, "Being" (*sat*), "Consciousness" (*cit*), and "Bliss or Rapture" (*ānanda*), which in anthropomorphic occidental terms would be, approximately, Father, Son, and Holy Spirit; Neoplatonically, (1) inheritance in the cause, (2) procession from the cause, and (3) reversion to the cause; and in Greek poetic imagery, the Graces.

In sum then, we may think of 3 as the liminal term of things apprehended in the field of space, time, and causality; what James Joyce in *Ulysses* (part 1, chapter 3, opening phrase) defines as the

"Ineluctable modality of the visible: at least that if no more. . . ." Augustine discerned the imprint of the Trinity in all things, regarding, however, the one essential Trinity as male, whereas the Greeks had a number of essential female trinities, for example, the Graces, the Hours, the Fates, and the Furies, as well as the great triad of the "Judgment of Paris," Aphrodite, Hera, and Athene.

Unquestionably, female triads long predated the historical appearance of Augustine's *trinitas* of three male personalities in one divine substance; for the mythologies of the great Neolithic goddesses—as the publications of Marija Gimbutas demonstrate— date back to the eighth millennium B.C.—at least! with antecedents even in the Paleolithic. Gimbutas calls attention, for example, to the late Paleolithic "Venus of Laussel" of ca. 20,000–18,000 B.C.[58] In a posture and with a gesture eloquent of some legend, the knowledge of which is irretrievably lost, this impressive little figure, carved in high relief on a limestone block discovered in a rock shelter from the period of the great painted caves of southern France and northern Spain, is of a corpulent, naked female, holding elevated in her raised right hand a bison horn on which thirteen vertical strokes are engraved, while caressing with her left hand her pregnant belly.[59] The figure must have represented some mythic personage so well known to the period that the reference of the elevated horn would have been as well known as, say, in India today, a lotus in the hand of the goddess Śri Lakshmī. Alexander Marshack in *The Roots of Civilization* remarks that "the count of thirteen is the number of crescent 'horns' that may make up an observational lunar year; it is also the number of days from the birth of the first crescent to just before the days of the mature full moon."[60] Filling the whole back wall of a shallow Paleolithic cave, from ca. 13,000 to ca. 11,000 B.C., at Angles-sur-Anglin (Vienne), there looms a large rock-carved composition of the great bellies, massive loins, and upper thighs of three colossal female presences, sexual triangles strongly marked, hovering as an immense triad above the horned head of a bull.[61] And some 10,000 years later, on a stone Gallo-Roman altar excavated from the site of the present Notre Dame de Paris and preserved in the basement of the nearby Musee de Cluny, there is carved the image of a bull beneath a tree upon which three cranes are to be seen. The inscription reads, *Tarvos Trigaranus,* "Bull with the Three Cranes," the crane being a bird symbolic at that time of the Celtic Triple Goddess.[62] "The sacredness of the bull," remarks Gimbutas in discussion of Neolithic symbolic forms, "is expressed in particular through the emphasis on horns. They are sometimes as large as the whole animal figurine. Replete with a mysterious power of growth, the horns have become a lunar symbol, which is presumed to have come into being in the Upper Paleolithic Aurignacian when reliefs of naked women holding a horn begin to appear.[63]

The magnificent female triad at Angles-sur-Anglin (Vienne), hovering above the horned head (or mask) of a bull, in what surely was a holy grotto, is (I believe) the earliest known representation of a triad of any kind in the history of art. The date, ca. 13,000–11,000 B.C., is some ten thousand years later than that of the Venus of Laussel, the Woman with the Horn. Another five thousand years and in Asia Minor, among the numerous shrines unearthed at Çatal Hüyük, a Neolithic town site elegantly published and illustrated by James Mellaart,[64] there are a number of female figures represented as giving birth to bulls; also, walls ornamented with triads of bull heads, as well as arrays of bull's horns, and an evident association, furthermore, of the symbol of the bull's head with the human cranium. Still another five thousand years, and at the island site in the river Seine of Notre Dame de Paris, that Gallo-Roman altar appeared of three cranes perched in a tree above the figure of a large standing bull.

The evidence is thus consistent, extensive, and unmistakable, of a prehistoric continuity of no less than twenty thousand years for a mythology of the female body as the matrix of what Plato in *Timaeus* referred to as "those states which affect moving and sensible things and of which generation is the cause . . . : the forms of time, which imitates eternity and revolves according to a law of number."

Already in the figure of the Venus of Laussel there is evidence of an interest in number; number associated, moreover, with the cycle of the moon, and the crescent moon associated with the horn or horns of a bull. The figure's left hand held to the belly suggests that a relationship had been already recognized between the female menstrual cycle and the waxing and waning of the moon—which in turn implies a dawning of the recognition of an identity of some kind, coordinating earthly and celestial numbers.

Marshack in *The Roots of Civilization* has demonstrated for the Upper Paleolithic an interest in day counts. Examining with a microscope the rows of notches carved in series along staves of horn, ivory, or bone, he found that in every case the successive notches had been carved by different instruments, presumably at different times, and he termed such artifacts "time factored." Moreover, since a significant number showed counts that matched lunar cycles, the possible inference followed of women keeping tally of their menstrual cycles in observation of the phases of the moon.

The phases of the moon are four: three visible (waxing, full, and waning) and one invisible (three nights dark). Persephone, ravished to the netherworld by Hades/Pluto, became—while there invisible to the living—queen of a netherworld of death and regeneration. Such an identification of the mystery of generation with death and sacrifice is, by analogy, in lunar imagery, associated with the fourth, the invisible phase, of the lunar cycle, which in the Eleusinian legend is equated with the night of the marriage of Persephone and Pluto. Classical representations of the triad of goddesses, Athene, Hera, and Aphrodite, at the scene of the Judgment of Paris show them attended by Hermes as a fourth, who, in fact, is the one who summons Paris to the confrontation. The two mythic episodes are of the same mythological vocabulary. And in both, the designation of a male-female *conjunctio* is related, one way or the other, to an association with the idea of a fourth in relation to a three.

The Angles-sur-Anglin triad, in association with the bull as a fourth, is a Paleolithic counterpart of the classical traid attended by Hermes. For as Marija Gimbutas points out, "The male god's principal epiphany was in the form of a bull." And as she remarks further, "A human head grafted onto a bull's body reaches a culmination of power through symbiosis: the wisdom and passions

98

of man merged with the physical strength and potency of the bull."[65] "The bull god was alive," she reminds us,

> in many areas of Greece and particularly in Macedonia in the time of Euripides whose *Bacchae* abounds in bull epiphanies:
>
> > *A Horned God was found*
> > *And a God with serpents crowned*
> > (Euripides, *Bacchae*, 99)
>
> In the Orphic mystery, the worshipper ate the raw flesh of the bull before he became "Bacchos." The ritual of Dionysus in Thrace included "bull-voiced" mimes who bellowed to the god. The scholiast on Lychophron's *Alexandra* says that the women who worshipped Dionysus Laphystion wore horns themselves, in imitation of the god, for he was imagined to be bull-headed and is so represented in art. . . . Dionysus also manifested himself as the bull Zagreus, in which guise he was torn to pieces by the Titans.[66]

The art of the Upper Paleolithic is the earliest art of which we have knowledge, providing our earliest pictorial evidence of mankind's mythic themes and actual ritual practices. The animal paintings in the stupendous temple caves had evidently to do with ceremonials of the hunt; probably also with the initiation of adolescents to manhood. The human figures represented are few and exclusively male, masked or semi-animal in form. The sculptural art of the numerous female figurines, on the other hand, is related generally to dwelling sites, and whereas in the caves the human figures are in action, performing ceremonials of one kind or another, the figurines are simply presentations in the nude of the female form. The little figures usually have no feet. A few have been found set standing upright in the earth of household shrines. Furthermore, in contrast to the shamanic figures in the caves, which seem to be always in the performance of their social functions, the female statuettes are not in action of any kind. They are simply there, in being, little presences in themselves, representations and reminders (for contemplation) of the mystery of the female body itself, which is, in fact, the sole source of the life and well-being of the very dwelling site in which the little figure will have been set standing.

In the exceptional example, from ca. 20,000 B.C., of the Woman with the Horn, discovered at one end of a long limestone ledge at Laussel, the essential features of the lunar mythology of which the figurines are expressions are unmistakably brought to view. And in the great triad at Angles-sur-Anglin (Vienne) the further mythological implications of these essential features are unfolded.

Normally, of course, it would be improper to suggest attributions to the figures from the twelfth millennium B.C. of ideas that become clear to us only from the first. However, when the vocabularies of two pictorial documents are visibly identical, it becomes difficult to argue that the artists in the first instance cannot have known what they were saying. Three female forms in association with a bull as the fourth! Three major goddesses in association with Hermes as a fourth! Three Graces ("the first moving thing") in association with Apollo as a fourth! Three visible phases of the waxing, full, and waning moon with the moon of the nights invisible as a fourth: the night's invisible being of the moon's apparent death and, then, resurrection! There is plenty of evidence that the people of the Upper Paleolithic understood very well the relationship of sexual intercourse to pregnancy. In the same site at Laussel at which the Woman with the Horn was found, there was also a sculptured representation of a couple in sexual union.[67] Since the elevated horn bearing thirteen strokes may be interpreted (as Marshack has suggested) as symbolic of the visibly waxing moon, while the woman's hand on her belly relates the phenomenon to that of the pregnant womb, there is surely an intention to be recognized in the appearance *in the same sanctuary* of a representation of what Freud and his school have called the "primal scene," which in terms of a lunar symbolic schedule is of the mystery of the fourth, the invisible phase.

Considering further the interesting triad at Angles-sur-Anglin, one cannot but notice that the sexual triangles are, all three, very well defined and that the mesial grooves are conspicuous. The triangles, furthermore, are distinctly equilateral, like the Pythagorean *tetraktys,* with the grooves then suggesting the point at the tetraktian apex as connoting the invisible source from which the visible form has proceeded—which is perhaps pressing the interpretation a bit too far; and yet, the analogy is impossible to miss. The triangle, furthermore, is the same as that which in Indian Tantric iconography is taken to connote the energy of the womb as identical with that of *maya.*

In the Paleolithic pictogram, the 3 triangles of 3 sides each announce, moreover, the number 9, which is that of the Muses manifesting in the field of space-time the energy (*vis*) of the Apollonian mind as mediated through the Graces—which is again, perhaps, pressing an interpretation too far; yet the number is conspicuously represented as of 3 mighty females hovering over the mask or head of a bull as a fourth—or, in relation to the 9, as a tenth. In relation to the Graces, Apollo appears as a fourth, and in relation to the Muses, as a tenth.

Now, whether allegorical thoughts of this kind can have been present in any way in the minds responsible for this masterwork—whether consciously, half-consciously, or unconsciously—who shall say? Many artists whom I know today are willing, even eager, to impute such mythological implications to their profoundly inspired productions when they learn of them from such scholars as myself. Psychoanalysts with their pudendascopes (James Joyce's word) readily discern intentions in works of art that no artist would have recognized. The method of mythology is analogy, and that the artists of the Paleolithic age were competent in analogy is surely evident in the statement of the Woman with the Horn, where a triple analogy is rendered of (1) the growing horns of a bull, (2) waxing crescent of the moon, and (3) growing child, *en ventre sa mère.*

The imagery of this art is derived, not only from accurate observation, but also from an unconditioned identification with the natural order. And the mythologies originating from that primal age were of the same disposition. The two modes, of art and of myth, therefore, not only supplemented each other, but also remained in accord with the root-being of phenomenal life, self-validated through the sense that they inspired of fulfillment.

By what coincidence of nature, however, can the numerology of the Paleolithic and Neolithic lunar reckoning of 3 + 3 + 3, as of the visible body of the universal Great Goddess, have been carried on, only amplified, in the Old Sumerian numerological reading of 4 + 3 + 2, to accord with an actual "Great," or "Platonic" Zodiacal cycle of 25,920 solar years, where 2 + 5 + 9 + 2 + 0 = 18, and 1 + 8 = 9, whose root, as Dante saw, is a trinity?

OF HARMONY AND OF DISCORD

In what has been called by some "The Heroic Age," of those centuries of barbaric invasions and wiping out of cities that we find celebrated in the Indo–European Iliad and Mahabharata, as well as throughout the Old Testament, there were brought onto the historic stage two sorts of nomadic, herding, and fighting peoples bearing analogous, though significantly differing, sociologically oriented systems of mythology inspired by notions of morality wherein the high concern was not of harmony with the universe in its mystery but of the aggrandisement and justification of some local, historical tribe or cult. The whole character, as well as function, of mythology was thereby transformed; and since the myths, ideals, and rites of the new orders of justified violence overlay wherever they fell the earlier of an essential peace at the heart of the universe, the history of mythology in a great quarter of the world for the past three thousand years has been of a double-layered continuum. In some parts, notably India, the mythology of the Goddess returned in time to the surface and even became dominant. Already at the conclusion of the Kena Upanishad (seventh century B.C., or so) there is described a notable and amusing scene, where the Indo–European Vedic gods are found powerless and are introduced to the knowledge of *brahman* by "a woman exceedingly beautiful, Uma, Daughter of the Mountain Himavat."[68] Also in Greece, the Great Goddess returned to power in many forms, most notably in the mysteries of Eleusis; and in the Near East as well, where a constant biblical refrain became of kings "who did evil in the sight of the Lord," as Solomon, for instance, who "went after Ashtoreth the goddess of the Sidonians, and after Milcom the abomination of the Ammonites . . . built a high place for Chemosh the abomination of Moab, and for Moloch the abomination of the Ammonites, on the mountain east of Jerusalem. And so he did for all his foreign wives, who burned incense and sacrifices to their gods" (1 Kings 11:5–8).

Read again the mad account of the rampage of the very good King Josiah of Judah (ca. 640–609 B.C.), when he

> deposed the idolatrous priests whom the kings of Judah had ordained to burn incense in the high places at the cities of Judah and round about Jerusalem; those also who burned incense to Ba'al, to the sun, and the moon, and the constellations, and all the host of the heavens. And he brought out the Asherah from the house of the Lord, outside Jerusalem, to the brook Kidron, and beat it to dust and cast the dust of it upon the graves of the common people. And he broke down the houses of the cult prostitutes which were in the house of the Lord, where the women wove hangings for the Asherah. And he brought all the priests out of the cities of Judah, and defiled the high places where the priests had burned incense, from Geba to Beersheba; and he broke down the high places of the gates that were at the entrance of the gate of Joshua the governor of the city, which were on one's left of the gate of the city. However, the priests of the high places did not come up to the altar of the Lord in Jerusalem, but they ate unleavened bread among their brethren. . . ." (2 Kings 23:5–9)

Thus the force of the underlying layer, even where officially suppressed or apparently forgotten, worked its influence, often in subtle ways; as for example, in the instance already recognized, of the number 86,400 concealed in the length of years of the biblical antediluvian age.

From as early as the fourth millennium B.C., the Indo-European, cattle-herding, patriarchal warrior tribes were overrunning and transforming the civilization of Europe.[69] Through centuries, waves of invasion followed waves, and with each there was carried into the field of world history another inflection of what Georges Dumézil has in many volumes represented as the prototypical structure of an Indo-European mythology, reflecting the tripartite class structure of a social order of farmers and cattle breeders under a leadership of battle-eager warrior-chiefs and magician-priests.[70]

In the Near East, very much the same was happening, as patriarchal, goat- and sheep-herding, Semitic tribes from the Syro-Arabian desert, under the leadership likewise of warrior-chiefs and magician-priests, were in the names of their gods consummating devastating victories over such long-established cities of the region as, for instance, Jericho (Joshua 6).[71] So that, as a consequence of all of this truly unspeakable violence and barbarity over an immense part of the already civilized portion of Europe and Asia (only Egypt on its desert- and god-protected Nile remained through those millennia unbroken), what the historian of mythologies everywhere uncovers, from the British Isles to the Gangetic Plain, is a consistent pattern (retained in religions even to the present day) of two completely contrary orders of mythic thought and symbolization flung together, imperfectly fused, and represented as though of one meaning.

The elder of the two, by far, was of the Neolithic Great Goddess, of whom the earliest known images, as recognized by Gimbutas, are of Old Europe, ca. 7000–3500 B.C., with antecedents, however, in the Upper Paleolithic period, going back to some 20,000, or more, B.C. And the critical point to be made here is that the interest of the earlier order of myth was emphatically in nature, and in the nature, specifically, of the female body as the giver of life and thus of one constitution with the universe. As bird, as fish, as duck, as deer, as frog, even as water, the Great Goddess appears: in many forms, if not already also of many names.

At which point it becomes perhaps appropriate to remark that in every lifetime there is indeed a period when the mother, and specifically the mother's female body, is, in fact, the universe. Indeed, it would be possible even to argue that the infant's initial experience of the mother as universe, transformed in later life into a sense of the universe as mother, should be recognized as the primal impulse of all mythological symbolization whatsoever.

In any case, in the art and arts of the Neolithic stage, not only of Old Europe but of the whole range known to us of peoples of the world, the *mysterium tremendum et fascinans* of life itself as motherhood and as birth, as growth and as transformation terminating in a return to the mother in death, out of which source appears new life, is universally, at this stage of civilization, the all-engrossing, first and last concern. I see no evidence anywhere among the remains of peoples at this stage of the development of civilization anything like the compulsion recognized by Dumézil in Indo-European mythology, to project upon the universe the conditions of their own social order. On the contrary, the compulsion is, rather, to adapt society to the conditions dictated by as much as can be understood of the universe.

And in the succeeding epoch of this biologically instructed, mother-goddess dominated tradition of mythological symbolization (that, namely, of the early Sumerian recognition, third millennium B.C. or so, of a mathematically controlled universal order of cycling eons of 43,200—432,000—or 4,320,000 years) the high concern was still to bring the now comparatively complex sociology of a constellation of agriculturally supported city-states into conformity with the order of the universe.

RAGNARÖK

The voice of the prophetess Völva, summoned by Othin to rise from the earth and discourse of the doom of the gods:

> On a hill there sat, and smote on his harp,
> Eggther the Joyous, the giants' warder;
> Above him the cock in the bird-wood crowed,
> Fair and red did Fjalar stand.
>
> Then to the gods crowed Gollinkambi,
> He wakes the heroes in Othin's hall;
> And beneath the earth does another crow,
> The rust-red bird at the bars of Hel.
>
> Now Garm howls loud before Gnipahellir,
> The fetters will burst, and the wolf run free;

Much do I know and more can see
Of the fate of the gods, the mighty in fight.

Brothers shall fight and fell each other,
And sisters' sons shall kinship stain;
Hard is it on earth, with mighty whoredom;
Axe-time, sword-time, shields are sundered,
Wind-time, wolf-time, ere the world falls;
Nor ever shall men each other spare.

Fast move the sons of Mim, and fate
Is heard in the note of the Gjallarhorn;
Loud blows Heimdall, the horn is aloft,
In fear quake all who on Hel's roads are.

Yggdrasil shakes, and shiver on high
The ancient limbs, and the giant is loose;
To the head of Mim does Othin give heed,
But the kinsmen of Surt shall slay him soon.

How fare the gods? how fare the elves?
All Jotunheim groans, the gods are at council;
Loud roar the dwarfs by the doors of stone,
Masters of the rocks, would you know yet more?

Now Garm howls loud before Gnipahellir,
The fetters will burst, and the wolf run free;
Much do I know, and more can see
Of the fate of the gods, the mighty in fight.[72]

The dissolution at the end of time of the shadow-play of the pairs-of-opposites: Armageddon, the biblical version of that day, of which Jesus also prophesied, when "brother will deliver up brother to death, and the father his child, and children will rise against parents and have them put to death," (Mark 13:12 et al.). Even the crowing of the cock, thrice, which Peter heard to his shame. . . . (Matt. 26:73–75; Mark 14:66–72, et al.)

On that day, the wolf Fenrir is to swallow the sun and with gaping mouth advance on the land, his lower jaw against the earth and upper against heaven. The World Ash, Yggdrasil, will tremble, trees shatter, crags fall to ruin. The sea will gush upon the

land, and the ship Naglfar (made of dead men's nails) steer land-
ward, bearing Loki aboard and the Rime-Giants. The Midgard
Serpent that surrounds the earth will be at Fenrir's side, blowing
venom, with all the champions of Hel following. And the heaven
will be cloven in their din.

Then Heimdallr, who sits at heaven's end guarding Bifrost, the
Rainbow Bridge (he sees equally well by night and by day, hears
the grass grow on earth and the wool on sheep, needs less sleep
than a bird, and sits snug in his hall, drinking gladly of good
mead), will sound mightily the Gjallarhorn; when the gods, all
waking, will in council meet, don war weeds, and venturing, 800
through each of Valhall's doors, 432,000 join the fiends of Hel in a
festival of mutual slaughter.[73]

"My hypothesis proposes," states the Icelander Einar Pálsson,
of his treatment in seven volumes of "The Roots of Icelandic
Culture,"[74] "that the world picture of pagan Iceland—the universe
of the Vikings—was the SAME as that of the Romans and the
Greeks, modified by time, a Nordic language and Christian cur-
rents. . . . What I have NOT found during 35 years of study into
the roots of Icelandic culture is anything which points to a separate
'Nordic' or even 'Germanic' religion in the sense that it is different
from that of the cultures of Sumer, Egypt, Greece and Rome."[75]

The Nordic settlement of the island during the six decades
A.D. 830–890 was by Viking families of two separate strains: a
Celtic Christian from the British Isles and a pagan directly from
Norway. Pálsson's recognition of a context of late classical (Neoplatonic) ideas in the Celtic Christianity of Iceland has been
recently corroborated archaeologically, by the sensational discovery at Dagvertharnes, in the west of Iceland, on the shores of the
Breithafjördur, or remains that have been described as "strongly
reminiscent of Celtic dwellings excavated in Britain," together
with "ten carved stones . . . including a pyramidal stone [a
tetrahedron] and what seems to be a stone cross."[76] The excavation
was conducted by the archaeologist Thorvaldur Fridriksson of the
University of Gothenburgh at a site that had been already identified by Pálsson as having the significance of the tetrahedron in

Celtic Christian ideology, namely, as connoting a hallowing in the settlement of land. The date as first announced was nearly two centuries too early but as corrected is in perfect accord with Pálsson's, after A.D. 870.

The Celtic Christianity which had been thus carried to Iceland was a direct continuation of the Mission of St. Patrick, the traditional date of whose arrival in the British Isles is A.D. 432 (!). The year before that date, at the Byzantine church council at Ephesus (the most important Near Eastern temple-city at that time of the Great Goddess of Many Names), Mary had been declared to be, indeed, *Theotókos,* the "Mother of God." And within half a century of that epochal date the Christian Roman Empire collapsed; all of Europe except Ireland was overrun by pagan Germanic tribes (Britain's invaders were the English); and for the next three to four centuries the task of re-Christianizing Britain and the Continent was the high concern of Irish monks. St. Columba's founding on the island of Iona, in the Inner Hebrides, A.D. 563, of a church and monastery dedicated to the pursuit of the work in Scotland, and the ambitious mission to Switzerland, Burgundy, and Italy of St. Columbanus with twelve companions, ca. 598–614, are the two best known of these undertakings. Two centuries later, at the court of Charles the Bald, near Laon, the Irish monk John Scotus Erigena (ca. 810–877) was translating out of Greek the writings of pseudo-Dionysius the Areopagite, St. Gregory of Nyasa, St. Epiphanius, and St. Maximus the Confessor, besides composing two philosophical treatises of his own: *De predestinatione* (in 851) and *De divisione naturae* (862–866), both of which were promptly condemned for implications, not only of pantheism, but also of reincarnation.

For the church of St. Peter, in Rome, had meanwhile recovered authority, and already in the year 664, at the Synod of Whitby in Northumbria, the Irish monks with their Neoplatonic theology based on the Book of Revelation and Gospel According to John, supported by their own mystical experiences in a tradition of meditation unmatched for severity save in India, had been required to retire from England, yielding to the Roman party the field which they there had tilled. Erigena's works, therefore, composed two centuries later, in the period just preceding the settlement of Iceland, was of a tradition which on the Continent had already gone underground, to be represented covertly in the symbolic language of alchemy and, most notably during the twelfth and early thirteenth centuries, in the Manichaean (Albigensian) heresy and the fundamentally Celtic legend of the Holy Grail. Not until Cosimo de' Medici's founding of his academy in Florence would the Greek language, bearing its heritage of Neoplatonic and Pythagorean thought, return to recognition in the Latin West.

What Erigena had preposed in his *De divisione naturae* was a reconciliation of the Christian doctrine of creation by a personal Creator-God with the Neoplatonic doctrine of emanation; a syncretization elegantly epitomized in his definition of four cosmogonic principles:

1. The uncreated creating
2. The created creating
3. The created uncreating
4. The uncreated uncreating

whereby the first and last are of God, as beginning and end, while the second and third are of the two modes of existence of created beings: the intelligible and the sensible. For man, according to this Gnostic view, is a microcosm of the universe: with his senses perceiving the sensible world, with reason examining its intelligible causes, and with the intellect knowing God. Through sin, the animal sensual nature predominates. With release from sin, the return to God begins; and with physical death, reunion with the uncreated.

Among the first of Erigena's Celtic Christian contemporaries to arrive in Iceland (as chronicled in the Landnámabók, "Book of the Claiming of the Land") were two brothers and a sister, who, sailing presumably from the Hebrides, put to shore along the south coast in the delta area now known as Landeyjar, "Land Islands," where there is a triple hill called Bergthórshvoll, which they evidently regarded as a holy spot. An earlier, pagan settler, Ketill hoengr by name, had already recognized, "claimed," and settled this whole part of the island.

109

In the western quarter, meanwhile, a second Christian company put to land in the neighborhood of Dagverthanes, where there have now been found the remains of what appears to have been a Celtic monastery. The leader of that group was Authr djúpúthga, widowed queen of King Oleifr the White of Dublinshire, a daughter of Ketill flatnefr, a chieftain of the Hebrides. Four of her brothers and sisters are named also as leading settlers of Iceland: Helgi bjólan (at Kjalarnes, near Reykjavík), Björn austraeni (at Snaefellsnes, in the middle west), Thórunn hyrna (at Eyjafjörthur, in the north), and Jórunn mannvitsbrekka (in the southeast, at Kirkjuber, where Landnáma states Christian Celtic hermits had lived before the advent of the Norsemen). Örlygr Hrappsson, a nephew of this family, brought up by a Bishop Patrick in the Hebrides, had been told by his bishop to settle where he would find "three stones raised upright,"[77] which suggests that Bishop Patrick must have had in mind a lithic monument already known from accounts of earlier Celtic Christians.

The appearance anywhere on the landscape of a suggestion of the number 3—in particular 3 rocks—was for these people a feature of significance, betokening a holy and appropriate site for Christian settlement. For the sense of the term *landnám*, "land claiming," was of a spiritual claiming as well as physical occupation of a newly discovered land. By recognizing in its natural conformations features symbolically suggestive, the settlers were enabled to inlay upon a *visible* landscape the outlines of an intelligible, otherwise invisible one, reminiscent of the mythology that they had brought with them in their heads; so that when the work was done, the whole of their settlement would have become for them an icon of the New Jerusalem.

And so we learn that some thirty miles inland, northeastward of the Landeyjar, there is a mountain showing 3 peaks, which was revered in the earliest period as a holy mountain by analogy with Golgotha and its three crosses: each cross to be associated with the five wounds of Christ, and the $5 \times 3 = 15$ wounds, with the 15 mysteries of his Virgin Mother Mary: 5 joyous mysteries (the Annunciation, Visitation, Nativity, Presentation in the Temple, and Finding of the Child Teaching in the Temple); 5 sorrowful mysteries (the Agony in the Garden of Gethsemane, Scourging, Crowning with Thorns, Carrying of the Cross, and the Crucifixion); 5 glorious mysteries (of the Resurrection, Ascension, Pentecostal Descent of the Holy Ghost upon the Apostles, Assumption of the Virgin Mary to Heaven, and her Coronation there by her Son).

The name, Thríhyrningur, of the holy mountain, means "Three Horn," which, according to Pálsson, may be understood also to mean "triangle." "Most modern Icelanders," he adds, "have taken it for granted that the name meant 'three peaks.'"[78] "Three Horn" suggests a lunar association, which in the earlier Celtic pagan period would have carried a reference to the great Celtic triple goddess of innumerable forms and names—Danu/Anu/Ana; Morrighan/Badhbh/Macha; and so on—who in folklore is known as Queen Mab of the ubiquitous Fairy Hills.

The Celtic imagination readily associates the silence of hills with the mystery of eternity (Erigena's "uncreated creating" and "uncreated uncreating"), out of which arise and appear the ephemera of space-time and back into which they disappear. A number of the best-known legends of the Middles Ages are of adventures into mountain fastnesses, those of Tannhauser in the *Venusberg,* for example, or of Parzival at the mountain-castle of the Grail. Pálsson points to an association of Mount Thríhyrningur with the Grail keeper and Grail legend.[79] Mythologically, such holy mountains have served as images symbolic of the *axis mundi,* that universal still point around which movement originates, and in every part of the ancient world they have been associated in this function with the being and presence of one or another of the forms of the Great Goddess: the might Cretan goddess on her mountaintop; Ki and Ninhursag of most ancient Sumer; Parvati in India, as the bride of Shiva and daughter of the snow-topped Himalaya. The image of the upward-pointing triangle is implicit in such a prominence, and this, in turn, suggests an association with the Pythagorean *tetraktys* and the upward-pointing tantric yantra, symbolic of the triad out of which the 9 unfolds, with a tenth point, the *bindu,* at the center.

The original abode of Ketill hoengr, the first *pagan* settler of the southern area, was at a site named Hof, meaning "Temple," which became then the point from which symbolic measurements of the land were counted. A line drawn northeast-southwest through Hof, toward the point, northeast, of midsummer sunrise (June 22, summer solstice), and the opposite point, southwest, of midwinter sunset (December 22, winter solstice, Yule or Christmas), extends northeast to a place called Stöng, the "Pole," the "Stick," or "Staff," and southwest, across and beyond the triple hill Bergthórshvoll, out to sea to a triple rock, Thrídrangar, uprising from a volcanic shelf that is still active and associated mythologically with the gate or portal to the timeless sphere of the *primum mobile,* or ninth heaven.[80]

Now from Bergthórshvoll to Stöng, the distance measured in Roman feet (as Pálsson has found) is 216,000 feet, or half of 432,000 (1 Roman foot = 29.69 cm: 216,000 Roman feet = approximately 64 kilometers, or 40 miles). At the center of this span is Steinkross, where presumably there was at one time a stone cross around which an immense geographical circle was envisioned, 216,000 Roman feet in diameter, as an earthly replica of the heavens.* Steinkross in the center was thus a counterpart of the pole star, the hub of the universe, while the circle itself, as a counterpart of the Zodiac, was divided in 12 "houses."

Known as the Wheel of Rangárhverfi, this schematic reflection of the heavens supplied the model for the spiritually grounded social organization that is represented in the original Icelandic constitution of A.D. 930, whereby a body of 36 "priest-kings," or Gothar, 3 to each of the 12 "houses," governed the island as at once its secular and spiritual authority. Kingship, in this view, had "a sacral character," as Pálsson declares, "it was part of the total universe . . . it reached unto the hidden depths of nature and the powers that rule nature. It was the king's function to 'maintain the harmony' of the integration between Man and the Cosmos."[81] Which, as we have already found, was the whole sense of the old

---

*Note that $216,000 = 60^3$, confirming Joseph Campbell's thesis with another Babylonian/sexagesimal affinity. *C.M.*

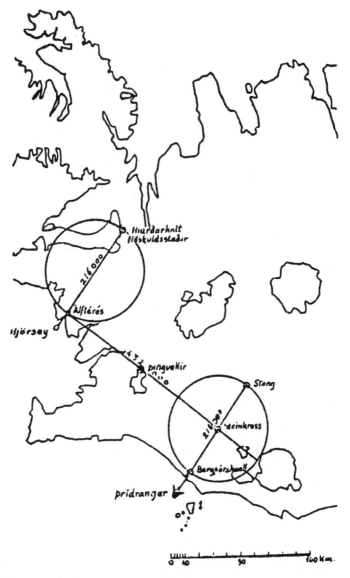

FIG. 4. Ketill Haengr's "Measuring Tree of the Universe," uniting the two original Icelandic settlements, south and west, showing Thingvellir between Steinkross and Álftárós, midway of a line of 432,000 Roman feet. Ninth century. Reconstruction by Einar Pálsson, *Raetur íslenzkrar menningar,* 7 vols. (1969–85).

113

Sumerian, as well as later Pythagorean, attention to the ordering mysteries of number.

From Steinkross, accordingly, a line projected 432,000 Roman feet northwestward touched the rim of a second symbolic circle, 216,000 Roman feet in diameter, by which the region was enclosed of the original, western, Celtic-Christian settlement. And precisely midway of this symbolic line, there is Thingvellir (a magnificent setting of volcanic landscape and adjacent plain), where the central place of assembly was fixed of the Althingi, the governing body politic of the whole inhabited quarter of the island.

The historical source of this concept of a society as a meso-cosmic coordinating force attuning human life to a natural order mathematically structured is not to be sought for in any of the primal Indo-European tribal pantheons, where, as Georges Dumézil has demonstrated, mythology and religion reflect the tripartite structural pattern of the basic Indo-European social hier-archy of (1) priests, (2) warriors, and (3) producers (cattle breeders and agriculturalists). What we here find, in contrast, is not a mythology reflecting the social order of a nomadic tribe, but a social order reflecting the Pythagorean concept of a mathematically structured macrocosm. For over a century and a half, Germanic scholarship has been arguing the opposed claims of those who interpret Germanic myth as a creation *sui generis* and those who view it as significantly influenced by Hellenistic and even early Christian models. Einar Pálsson's uncovering in ninth- and tenth-century Iceland of the indubitable signs of a mathematically struc-tured Pythagorean philosophical ground that was identical in all essentials with that of Cosimo de' Medici's fifteenth-century Flor-entine academy confirms the case, once and for all, of those who— with Alfons Dopsch, *Wirtschaftliche und soziale Grundlagen der europäischen Kulturentwicklung aus der Zeit von Caesar bis auf Karl den Grossen* (2 vols. [Vienna, 1918–20; 2d ed., 1923–24]), and Franz Rolf Schröder, *Germanentum und Hellenismus* (Heidelberg, 1924), *Die Parzivalfrage* (München, 1928, *Altgermanische Kulturprobleme* (Berlin, Leipzig, 1929)—had recognized that for centuries the Ger-mans had been profoundly in touch with and influenced by the civilizations of Greece, Rome, and the Near East.

Specifically, the chief centers of contact were in the West, along the Rhine, where, from the period of Caesar's conquest of Gaul, continuous Gallo–Roman influences, first pagan, then Christian, played into the German culture-field, and in the East, the north shore of the Black Sea, where, from no later than the second century A.D., the Goths were sharing with Iranians and Greeks the rich heritage of Hellenistic art, science, philosophy, and religion. By the fourth century A.D., until shattered ca. 370 by the Huns, a Gothic empire extended from the Black Sea to the Baltic. Ulfila's fourth-century translation of the Bible into Gothic was made for the Visigoths along the lower Danube. There exist fragments of a Gothic commentary on the John Gospel, as well as of an exchange of letters concerning textual interpretations between Gothic Christians (who were of the Arian heresy) and Hieronymus (St. Jerome, ca. 347–419). Schröder calls attention, also, to a discovery in the Egyptian desert of a bilingual (Gothic/Latin) page from the Bible, possibly of a Gothic officer in the Roman army; or if later, in the period of the Christian empire, either an Arian heretic in exile or some Gothic monk who had retired in meditation to the desert.

Even earlier than the Gothic East, the Christian mission had flourished in the Rhineland. There were established sees in Treves, Metz, and Cologne already in the third century. Moreover, nearly all of the pagan, classical and Oriental, mystery religions had been by that time long established and flourishing in both the Gallo-Roman and Germano-Roman zones. Egyptian Isis and Serapis, Syrian Attis and Cybele, Persian Mithra, Thracian Sabazius, Orpheus, Jupiter, Dolichenus, and many others were represented. Entire communities had exchanged their native deities for these, in whose worship they experienced profounder satisfactions. And the native cults themselves had meanwhile been gradually transformed by influences from these sources.[83]

> I ween that I hung on the windy tree,
>   Hung there for nights full nine;
> With spear I was wounded, and offered I was
>   To Othin, myself to myself,
> On the tree that none may ever know
>   What root beneath it runs.

None made me happy with loaf or horn,
  And there below I looked;
I took up the runes, shrieking I took them,
  And forthwith back I fell.

Then began I to thrive, and wisdom to get,
  I grew and well I was;
Each word led me on to another word,
  Each deed to another deed.[84]

What has been described as the "Christian-Pagan Syncretism" of the earlier Middle Ages—antecedent to (or, as in Iceland, beyond the ban of) the intolerant creedal edict of Theodosius I the Great (issued February 28, 380; confirmed 381, at the second ecumenical council, ten years before the burning of the Alexandrian *Mouseion*)—is explicit in this image of Othin, hung 9 nights on the "windy tree" of the World Ash Yggdrasil (Christ, 3 hours on Holy Rood); a sacrifice, himself to himself (the Son to his consubstantial Father); pierced by the Lance (of Longinus). Identified with Mercury, Othin (Wodan) was named as tutelary of the fourth day of the Alexandrian planetary week, in the series, Sol, Luna, Mars, Mercurius (= Wednesday: Wodan's day), Jupiter, Venus, and Saturn, and was thus identified, not only with the crucified Christ, but also with Hermes/Mercury/Thoth, Hellenistic Hermes Trismegistus (patron of the hermetic sciences, alchemy and the like) as well as with a celestial sphere.

Similarly, in the Irish Book of Kells (late eighth to early ninth century), the symbolically illuminated, so-called *Tunc* page, bearing the text of Matt. 27:38 (*Tunc crucifixerant XRI cum eo duos latrones,* "Then there were crucified with him two thieves"), adds to the idea of the crucified Christ a number of mythological themes of a distinctly pagan, Neoplatonic, and perhaps even Oriental tantric cast. The "ornamental animal style" of the illumination itself is identical, for example, with that of the pagan Norse, which in turn is but the northern reflex of an Old Germanic development of a Sarmatian-Scythian animal style of the Gothic Black Sea domain, the origins of which have been traced, on one hand, through Assyria back to Sumer and, on the other hand, into

FIG. 5. *Tunc* page of the Book of Kells: *Tunc crucifixerant XRI cum eo duos latrones* (Matt. 27:38). Ireland, Ninth century. Trinity College Library, Dublin. Drawing by John Mackay.

Turkestan, whence, when carried eastward, it evolved into the animal style of Shang China.[85] It is therefore not by coincidence (or by what anthropologists call "convergence") that the same dual and triple yin-yang symbols that appear on the heads of two drums flanking the altar in Tokyo of the Shinto Yasukuni Shrine (dedicated to the Japanese war-dead) also appear on certain pages of the Book of Kells.

The all-enclosing, feline-headed serpent of the *Tunc* page, shown swallowing fire from its own tail, is a counterpart of the Norse Midgard Serpent as the bounding power of the macrocosm, both as space (water) and as time (fire). Plato, in *Timaeus,* in his bewildering discussion of the four elements, identifies fire with the form of the tetrahedral pyramid (*Timaeus* 55b) and writes of fire as the beginning and end of creation. So we find it here represented as at the beginning and end of an eon. The discovery in Iceland of a stone pyramid among the remains of what appears to have been a Celtic-Christian monastery confirms what Pálsson had already predicted as a likely symbolic form to be found associated with such a site, signifying creation by fire, destruction by fire, the end of one era, the beginning of another, and the hallowing by fire of the land.

The all-enclosing serpent's folds support 3 panels containing 5 persons each, recalling the $3 \times 5 = 15$ crosses that are in Iceland associated with the 3 summits of Mount Thríhyrningur and the 5 joyous, 5 sorrowful, and 5 glorious mysteries of the Virgin; while the convoluted animal at the head of the page, representing Christ as a microcosm, matching the macrocosmic uroboros, appears to be either swallowing or disgorging two animal-headed snakes, one with the head of a fox, the other, of a cat. In color, one is blue, the other, red. Can these possibly correspond to the *ida* and *pingala* nerves of the tantric lunar and solar breaths?

In Monasterboice (county Louth) there is a monumental Irish stone cross known as the Cross of the Abbot Muirdach (who died in 844), which bears on one side a caduceus-like engraving of two serpents, one upward turned, the other downward, whose interlacing coils enframe three human heads (such as might refer to Chakras 4, 5, and 6), and with a large human right hand above,

FIG. 6 *Dextra Dei*. Cross of Muiredach, Monasterboice, Ireland, Tenth century.

reaching up to rest upon a halo.[86] Known as *Dextra Dei,* "the Right Hand of God," such an ornament appearing on the cross of Christ Crucified cannot have been without meaning. But who shall now say what the meaning might have been?

Othin hung 9 days on the "windy tree," by virtue of which sacrifice he gained knowledge of the runes: Christ, 3 hours on Holy Rood, by virtue of which sacrifice he gained for mankind redemption from the mortal effects of the sin of Adam and Eve. Elaine Pagels, in her illuminated and illuminating book *The Gnostic Gospels,* interpreting a body of Jewish and Christian Gnostic texts recently discovered in a ceramic jar unearthed from the Egyptian desert (where it had been buried for preservation, apparently, about the time of the destruction of the Alexandrian *Mouseion*), points out that the gospel of the Gnostic Jesus, like that of Gautama Buddha, had to do, not with sin and redemption, but with illusion and enlightenment (*māyā* and *bodhi*).[87]

Othin sacrificed one eye for knowledge of the runes. One socket ever thereafter gazed inward, the other, ever outward, held to the world of phenomenality. The two interlacing snakes, red and blue, of the *Tunc* page of the Book of Kells are evidently of like meaning: one, of the knowledge inward of eternal life, the other, outward, of temporality; in tantric terms, respectively, "solar" consciousness (the nerve *piṅgalā*) and "lunar" consciousness (the nerve *iḍā*), the "still point" and the "turning world," *nirvāṇa* and *saṁsāra,* which are to be known in the way of one "released while living" (*jīvan mukta*) as one and the same, *nirdvandva,* nondual.

This is the mystery symbolized in its simplest geometrical form as a dot in the center of a circle; also, as a dot in the center of a triangle; or, as Gimbutas found in her Neolithic goddess figurines, a dot within a lozenge of four angles. The Christian designation in the year 431 of Mary as *Theotókos,* the very Mother of God, represents the continuation into a later, patriarchal context of this same idea of a nondual goddess–creator of the gods and all things, "bisexual, absolute and single in her generative role," creating (like the spider its web) her world from her own substance. The idea is represented in Indian (Jaina) art in the image of the universe as of a woman's form, with the earthly plane at the level of her waist, heavens in series to the crown of her head, and purgatories to the soles of her feet.

In the Musée de Cluny, in Paris, there is a lovely little *Vierge Ouvrante* of the young mother seated with the Christ Child on her arm.[88] Her body can be opened as a cabinet to reveal a vision within, not only of her son already crucified, but also of the visage of God the Father, as well as God the Holy Ghost as a dove, together with the heavenly choir of saints and angels. And from the same period, in the late-medieval (Marseilles) Tarot deck (of which the earliest preserved examples are from an elegent deck prepared about 1392 by the artist Jacquemin Gringonneur for King Charles VI of France), the culminating symbolic image, displayed on trump card number 21, is of "The World," *Le Monde,* as a dancing nude female (the alchemical female androgyne), framed in a mandorla of 3 colors, yellow, red, and blue (Father, Son, and Holy Ghost), and showing in each of the card's 4 corners one of the Zodiacal signs of the 4 Evangelists. Compare the twelfth-century west portal of Chartres cathedral, where, however, it is not the dancing Goddess Universe who thus appears as the culminating spiritual symbol but Christ of the Second Coming, at the end of time.

Two contrary points of view are represented in this contrast: that of the eye and mind of phenomenality and temporality, anticipating the end of the world as a historical event, and that of the Gnostic transformation of consciousness, whereby the world as normally perceived dissolves in the way of Blake's realization announced in *The Marriage of Heaven and Hell:* "If the doors of perception were cleansed every thing would appear to man as it is, infinite." We find a similar statement of Jesus in the Gnostic *Gospel According to Thomas* (which, like a jinni of the Arabian Nights, has come out of that buried Egyptian jar): "His disciples said to him: When will the Kingdom come? Jesus said: It will not come by expectation; they will not say: 'See, here,' or 'See, there.' But the Kingdom of the Father is spread upon the earth and men do not see it" (Logion 113). And again: "For the Kingdom is within you and it is without you" (Logion 3).[89]

Othin, by virtue of his sacrifice of one eye, therefore, was enabled to summon from the earth an apparition of the prophetess, from whom he learned not only of the end of his eon of 432,000 years but also of the whereabouts of both the Gjallarhorn (by whose sounding the moment of dissolution was to be announced) and the eye that he had given in pledge to Mimir, spirit of the waters, for the gift of insight.

> I know the horn of Heimdallr, hidden
> Under the high-reaching holy tree;
> On it there pours from Valfather's pledge
> A mighty stream: would you know yet more?
>
> Othin, I know where thine eye is hidden,
> Deep in the wide-famed well of Mimir;
> Mead from the pledge of Othin each morn
> Does Mimir drink: would you know yet more?[90]

The sounding of the Gjallarhorn is to be understood in Gnostic/Pythagorean terms as the harbinger of an awakening, and Heimdallr, from whose breath the tone proceeds, is the Awakener. "He is called the White God," says Snorri. "He is great and holy; 9 maids, all sisters, bore him for a son [compare the 9 Muses with Apollo as a 10th]. He is called also Hallinskidi [the "Ram"] and Gullintanni ["Golden Teeth"]; his teeth were of gold; his horse's name is Gold-top; and he dwells hard by Bifrost [the rainbow bridge from earth to Valhall], in the place called Himinbjorg [Heaven-mount]."[91]

He is, in other words, the Nordic Anthropos. Schröder likens him to Mithra, the Iranian lord of the victory of light, born the night of the winter solstice from a virgin mother rock.[92] One may liken him also to Christ, the "Sacrificial Lamb" or "Ram," born that same night of his virgin mother in a cave. The implied association of Heimdallr as Ram is with the first sign, Aries, of the Zodiac and the spring equinox, namely, Easter. Pálsson makes the point, quoting as authority Ernest G. McClain in *The Myth of Invariance,* that Claudius Ptolemaeus (fl. in Alexandria, A.D. 127–148), correlated the 12 signs of the zodiac with the 15 of the Greek 2-octave "Greater Perfect System" in such a way that the

Ram (Aries) stood for the ground tone, *Proslambanomene* (see Gafurius's chart, fig. 2,) as well as the "limiting tone," *Nete hyperbolaion,* two octaves higher.[93]

Now, in the Pythagorean reckoning, the number of vibrations of Middle-A, *Proslambanomene,* is 432 (modern tunings are generally higher). One octave lower is 216; two octaves lower, 108. These are all numbers of the Great Goddess, born, so to say, out of 9.

"At the end and presumably at the beginning of the world," states Pálsson, "Heimdallr blows his horn. . . . The sybil knows where the sound of Heimdallr is hidden:

> Under the high-reaching tree.
> The sound of Heimdallr is hidden under the measuring rod of the universe . . . the Ash Yggdrasil. . . .
> Voluspa clearly gives one to understand that the sound resounds in the old tree:
>> Yggdrasil shakes, and shiver on high
>> The ancient limbs.

"It would seem the ancients knew," Pálsson continues, "that a certain note causes a thing to resound through the same number of vibrations in an object. If so, it would give a perfect answer to the question why the Ash resounds ("ymr") when Heimdallr blows his horn. It is the resonance of the numbers 108–216–432 which defines the physical world from beginning to end."[94]

Let us here recall the idea already noted from the Indian Vedas of sound, *śabda,* as generator of the perceived universe. "It shouts out the universe, which is not distinct from itself. . . . This is how it is *nāda,* 'vibration.' This is what is meant by the saying: 'Sound (*śabda*), which is of the nature of *nāda,* resides in all living beings.'" And from the Confucian philosopher, Tung Chung-shu: "Tuned to the tone of Heaven and Earth, the vital spirits of man express all the tremors of Heaven and Earth, exactly as several citharas, all tuned on *Kung* [the tonic], all vibrate when the note Kung resounds. The fact of the harmony between Heaven and Earth and Man does not come from a physical union, from a direct action, it comes from a tuning on the same note producing vibrations in unison. . . . In the universe there is no hazard, there is no spontaneity; all is influence and harmony, accord answering accord."[95] Which is exactly what in the West is known as the Harmony of the Spheres, as represented in Gafurius's design by the lute held extended in Apollo's left hand while his right points to the Graces.

And so we find, indeed, as Pálsson has claimed, that "the world picture of pagan Iceland—the universe of the Vikings—was the SAME as that of the Romans and the Greeks." It was the same as that of India and China as well: a world picture of harmony and accord in the living body of a Mother Universe, who, as Marija Gimbutas's work has shown, was represented in the earliest Neolithic arts of Old Europe, 7000–3500 B.C., as the one "Great Goddess of Life, Death, and Regeneration."

The recognition of a mathematical regularity of $60 \times 432 = 25{,}920$ years in the pulse throughout the body of this universal being (as it were, the great diastole and systole of her heart), which appears to have been first registered in Sumer, ca. 3500 B.C., had by 1500 B.C. given rise, from the Nile and Tigris-Euphrates to the Indus and Huang-ho, to four structurally homologous, monumental civilizations, shaped to mythologies metaphorical of a sublime indwelling life informing all things; which in the sixth century B.C. became associated by Pythagoras (a Greek contemporary of the Buddha) with the mathematical laws at once of music, geometry, astronomy, and meditation.

Both the pagan Nordic and early Celtic-Christian theologies of Europe were informed by the scientistic insights of this fundamentally Gnostic, Pythagorean way of understanding and symbolization, which elsewhere in the Latin West was systematically and most viciously suppressed by the champions of a historical institution that James Joyce has somewhere characterized as a "conspiracy of morbid bachelors." Irrepressibly, notwithstanding, the larger view from time to time broke through—in the Celtic, Pelagian heresy, Scotus Erigina's ruminations, Arthurian romance, the Grail legend, even the fortune-telling Tarot deck. In Dante's *Divina Commedia* it is boldly represented, and in the Neoplatonic Florentine academy of the Medicis it gained the field—simply by way of a recognition that all the forms of theological discourse are meta-phorical of spiritual values, not to be understood as things-in-themselves.

"Man's last and highest leave-taking," declared the mystic Meister Eckhart, "is leaving God for God,"[96] leaving the histor-ically conditioned idea of God of one's faith for "that [to quote the Upanishad] to which speech goes not, nor the mind" (Kena 1.3). Within the field of mythic thought, however, both metaphorically (as one's nature knows) and historically (as Gimbutas[97] shows) the God beyond God is God's Mother.[98]

Notes

1. Grimnismäl 23, translated by Henry Adams Bellows, *The Poetic Edda* (American-Scandanavian Foundation, Oxford University Press, 1923), 93.

2. Völuspá, 59–62; Bellows, *Poetic Edda,* 24–25, abridged.

3. The recognition of this number in the Book of Revelation I owe to the Icelandic scholar Einar Pálsson, whose *Roetur íslenskrar menningar,* (*The Roots of Icelandic Cuture,* 7 vols. [Reykjavík: Mímir, 1969–85]) argues that the culture of Pagan/Celtic–Christian Iceland during the period ca. A.D. 870–1000 was of a piece with that of contemporary medieval Europe and not, as has been commonly supposed, of a separate and distinct, specifically Nordic source and context. His argument has been summarized in English in three brief monographs: *The Dome of Heaven: The Marking of Sacred Sites in Pagan Iceland and Medieval Florence* (Reykjavík: Mímir, 1981), *Hypothesis as a Tool in Mythology,* (Mímir, 1984), and *Celtic Christianity in Pagan Iceland* (Mímir, 1985).

4. For this dating of the tablet, see Samuel Noah Kramer, *Sumerian Mythology* (Philadelphia: American Philosophical Society, 1944), 9.

5. I have followed primarily Arno Poebel, *Historical Texts* (Philadelphia: University Museum, Publications of the Babylonian Section, vol. 4, no. 1, 1914), 17–20, but with considerable help from the later renditions by Stephen Herbert Langdon, *Semitic Mythology,* vol. 5 of *The Mythology of All Races,* 13 vols. (Boston: Marshall Jones, 1931), 17–20, and Samuel Noah Kramer, *From the Tablets of Sumer* (Indian Hills, CO: Falcon's Wing Press, 1956), 179–81.

6. Julius (Jules) Oppert, "Die Daten der Genesis," *Königliche Gesellschaft der Wissenschaften zu Göttingen,* Nachrichten, no. 10 (May 1877): 201–27.

7. Samuel Noah Kramer, *The Sumerians* (Chicago: University of Chicago Press, 1963), 42.

8. Ibid., 59.

9. Ibid., 59–68.

10. Ibid., 144–45.

11. Ibid., 42.

12. Alain Daniélou, *Shiva et Dionysos* (Paris: Librairie Artheme Fayard, 1982); English translation by K. F. Hurry, *Shiva and Dionysus* (New York: Inner Traditions International, 1984), 20–23.

13. Kramer, *Sumerians,* 40–41.

14. Marija Gimbutas, *The Goddesses and Gods of Old Europe, 7000–3500* B.C. (Berkeley and Los Angeles: University of California Press, 1974), 195.

15. Ibid., 196.

16. Daniélou, *Shiva and Dionysus,* 32.

17. Apuleius, *The Golden Ass,* translated by W. Adlington, book 11.

18. Kramer, *Sumerians,* 122.

19. *The Gospel of Sri Ramakrishna,* translated by Swami Nikhilananda (New York: Ramakrishna-Vivekananda Center, 1942), 336.

20. Gimbutas, *Goddesses and Gods,* 196.

21. *Muṇḍaka Upanishad* 1.1.7.

22. *Vedāntasāra* 56.

23. Gimbutas, *Goddesses and Gods,* 38.

24. Ibid., 89.

25. Ibid., 236.

26. Ibid., 19–34.

27. Ibid., 85–87.

28. Kramer, *Sumerians,* 93.

29. Ibid., 94.

30. Kenneth H. Cooper, M.D., M.P.H., *Aerobics* (New York: Bantam Books, 1968), 101.

31. Arthur Avalon (Sir John Woodroffe), *The Serpent Power,* 3d rev. ed. (Madras: Ganesh, 1931), 215.

32. H. V. Hilprecht, *The Babylonian Expedition of the University of Pennsylvania, Series A: Cuneiform Texts,* vol. 20, pt. 1 (University of Pennsylvania, University Museum, 1906), 31.

33. Alfred Jeremias, *Das Alter der babylonischen Astronomie* (Leipzig: J. C. Hinrechs'sche Buchhandlung, 2 Aufl., 1909), 68, note 1.

34. Ibid., 71–72.

35. D. R. Dicks, *Early Greek Astronomy to Aristotle* (Ithaca, NY: Cornell University Press, 1970), 62–63.

36. Alain Daniélou, *Introduction to the Study of Musical Scales* (London: India Society, 1943), 7. Text italics, mine.

37. *Li Chi* 28.97–99, translated by Derk Bodde, in Fung Yu-lan, *A History of Chinese Philosophy,* 2 vols. (Princeton: Princeton University Press, 1952), 1:343.

38. Tung Chung-shu, translated by Daniélou, *Introduction to the Study of Musical Scales*, 6–7, André Preau, "Lie Tseu," in *La Voile d'Isis* (Paris: Chacornac), no. 152–53 (1932), 554–55.

39. Daniélou, *Introduction to the Study of Musical Scales*, 12.

40. Tao Te Ching 42, translated by James Legge, *Sacred Books of the East*, edited by F Max Muller, vol. 39, *The Texts of Taoism*, part 1, p. 85.

41. *La Vita Nuova* II, III and XXX, abridged, translated by Charles Eliot Norton, *The New Life of Dante Alighieri* (Boston and New York: Houghton Mifflin, 1967), 1–2, 3–4, and 65–66.

42. Gimbutas, *Goddesses and Gods*, 205.

43. *Theogony* 116–34, abridged, translated by Richard Lattimore, *Hesiod* (Ann Arbor: University of Michigan Press, 1959), 130–31.

44. See *The Jerusalem Bible* (Garden City, N.Y.: Doubleday, Imprimatur, 1966), 943, note h.

45. Dom Gaspar LeFebure O.S.B., *Daily Missal with Vespers for Sundays and Feasts* (Lophem-near-Bruges, Belgium: Abbey of St. Andre; Saint Paul Minnesota: The R.M. Lohmann Co., 1934), 187.

46. These are recorded in Asoka's Rock Edict XIII. Cf. Vincent A. Smith, *The Edicts of Asoka* (London, 1909), 20. This is an exceedingly rare book, only one hundred copies having been printed. It revises the translations given by the author in his earlier volume, *Asoka: The Buddhist Emperor of India* (Oxford, 1901).

47. *Conclusiones . . . de modo intelligendi hymnos Orphei*, no. 8, as cited by Edgar Wind, *Pagan Mysteries in the Renaissance*, rev. and enlarged ed. (New York and London: W. W. Norton, 1968), 36.

48. Wind, *Pagan Mysteries*, 36.

49. Ibid., 37–38 and note 9.

50. Wind, *Pagan Mysteries*, 259.

51. Ibid., 266.

52. Shatcakranirūpanam 49; Avalon, *The Serpent Power*, 448.

53. Wind, *Pagan Mysteries*, 38, note 9, citing Proclus, *Elements of Theology*, prop. 35 (ed. Dodds [1933], 18f).

54. Wind, *Pagan Mysteries*, p. 38, note 9.

55. Ibid., 43.

56. Translation by J. L. Stocks, in *The Complete Works of Aristotle*, edited by Jonathan Barnes, Bollingen Series LXXI> 2 (Princeton: Princeton University Press, 1984), 1:447.

57. B. Jowett translation, 4th ed., revised, 1953; 1st ed., 1871.

58. Gimbutas, *Goddesses and Gods*, 93.

59. Joseph Campbell, *The Way of the Animal Powers*, vol. 1 of *Historical Atlas of World Mythology* (New York and San Francisco: Harper & Row, Alfred van der Marck editions, 1983). See figs. 66 and 109, "The Woman with the Horn."

60. Alexander Marshack, *The Roots of Civilization* (New York: McGraw-Hill, 1972), 335 and note 17.

61. Campbell, *Animal Powers,* fig. 111.

62. Ibid., fig. 112.

63. Gimbutas, *Goddesses and Gods,* 93.

64. James Mellaart, *Çatal Hüyük: A Neolithic Town in Anatolia* (New York: McGraw-Hill, 1967).

65. Gimbutas, *Goddesses and Gods,* 224.

66. Ibid., 227.

67. Campbell, *Animal Powers,* fig. 110.

68. Kena Upanishad 3–4.

69. See Marija Gimbutas's fundamental articles on this subject in *The Journal of Indo-European Studies,* vol. 1, no. 1 (Spring 1973), "Old Europe c. 7000–3500 B.C.: The Earliest European Civilization before the Infiltration of the Indo-European Peoples"; and vol. 1, no. 2 (Summer 1973), "The Beginning of the Bronze Age in Europe and the Indo-Europeans 3500–2500 B.C."; also, vol. 8, nos. 3 and 4 (Fall/Winter 1980), "The Kurgan wave #2 (c. 3400–3200 B.C.) into Europe and the Following Transformation of Culture."

70. For an introduction to the works and career of Georges Dumézil, see Edgar C. Polomé, ed., "Homage to Georges Dumézil," *Journal of Indo-European Studies,* monograph no. 3 (1982).

71. The earliest archaeological strata of this important site date back to ca. 8000 B.C. See Kathleen M. Kenyon, *Archaeology in the Holy Land* (New York: Frederick A. Praeger, 1960), 42.

72. Völuspá 42–49; translated by Bellows, *Poetic Edda,* 18–21.

73. Snorri Sturluson, "The Beguiling of Gylfi" 51; adapted from Arthur Gilchrist Brodeur, *The Prose Edda of Snorri Sturluson* (New York: American-Scandinavian Foundation, Oxford University Press, 1929), 77–81.

74. Einar Pálsson, *Roetur íslenzkrar menningar,* 7 vols., more to come (Reykjavík: Mímir, 1969–85).

75. Einar Pálsson, *Hypothesis as a Tool in Mythology* (Reykjavík: Mímir, 1984), 11.

76. As reported in *News from Iceland,* Reykjavík (August 1985): 1, 22; Also, Morgunblathith (July 16, 1985), 52.

77. Einar Pálsson, *Celtic Christianity in Pagan Iceland* (Reykjavík: Mímir, March 1985), 22–23.

78. Pálsson, *Hypothesis as a Tool in Mythology,* 24.

79. Pálsson, *Celtic Christianity in Pagan Iceland,* 8–9.

80. Einar Pálsson, *The Dome of Heaven: The Marking of Sacred Sites in Pagan Iceland and Medieval Florence, A Report on Studies in Florence in May 1980* (Reykjavík: Mímir, April 1981), 47.

81. Pálsson, *Celtic Christianity in Pagan Iceland,* 7.

82. Franz Rolf Schröder, *Altgermanische Kulturprobleme,* Trübners Philologische Bibliothek Band 11 (Berlin und Leipzig: Walter de Gruyter, 1929), 64.

83. Ibid., 69–70.

84. Hávamál 139, 140, 142, translated by Bellows, *Poetic Edda,* 60–61.

85. A critical review of the scholarship of this subject appears in Schröder, *Altgermanische Kulturprobleme,* 21–39.

86. Campbell, *The Mythic Image,* fig. 308.

87. Elaine Pagels, *The Gnostic Gospels* (New York: Random House, 1979), xx and *passim.*

88. Campbell, *Mythic Image,* figs. 53 and 54.

89. *The Gospel According to Thomas,* Coptic text established and translated by A. Guillaumont, H.-Ch. Puech, G. Quispel, W. Till, and Yasah abd al Masih (Leiden: E. J. Brill; New York: Harper & Brothers, 1959), 55, 57, and 3.

90. Völuspá 27 and 28/29 combined and abridged. Bellows, *Poetic Edda,* 12–13.

91. Snorri Sturluson, Gylfaginning 27. Brodeur, *The Prose of Edda of Snorri Sturluson,* 40.

92. Schröder, *Altgermanische Kulturprobleme,* chap. 17.

93. Pálsson, *Hypothesis as a Tool in Mythology,* 31, citing Ernest G. McClain, *The Myth of Invariance* (New York: Nicolas Hays, 1976), 104–5.

94. Ibid., 32–35.

95. Quotations from Daniélou, *Introduction to the Musical Scales,* as cited earlier.

96. Sermon on "Riddance" in Franz Pfeiffer, *Meister Eckhart,* translated by C. de B. Evans, 2 vols. (London: John M. Watkins, 1947), sermon 96, vol. 1, p. 239.

97. And others, most notable among whom are Johann Bachofen (*Matriarchy and Primordial Religion* [*Mutterrecht und Urreligion,* 1861]); Hermann Wirth ("Die Symbolhistorische Methode," in *Zeitschrift f. Religionswissenschaft* [Münster, 1955]); Louise Hagberg (*Easter Eggs and their Pre-Christian Origin* [Fataburen 1906]); and Franz Hancar ("The Problem of the Venus-statuettes in the Eurasian Paleolithic" in *Praehistorische Zeitschrift,* 30–31 [1939–40]: 128). Hermann Wirth cites Hancar and was the first to note as far back as 1955 that "these cultic birds with their symbolic ornaments are the same companion birds of a fully stylized statuette of the Great Mother-Goddess, the 'Stara Baba' [i.e., "Ancient Mother," *C.M.*] of Siberia as found at Kostyenki and Gagarino in the Don region, as well as around Willendorf in lower Austria: statuettes related also to the southwestern mother-goddess statues of Menton, Brassempouy and Laussel." *C. M.*

98. Ancient Egypt would put this unambiguously as "The Horus beyond Osiris is Isis, Mother of Horus"—"Osiris" and "Horus" denoting two stages in the growth of divinity. *C. M.*

4

THE AGELESS WAY
OF GODDESS
Divine Pregnancy and Higher Birth
in Ancient Egypt and China

CHARLES MUSÈS

Though both are related to it, the point of shamanism is really not ecstasy, "archaic" or otherwise, or even "healing," but rather the development of communication with a community of higher than human beings and a modus operandi for attaining an eventual transmutation to more exalted states and powers. Those whom that goal does not attract, authentic shamanism does not address.

The point is *theurgy,* literally a divine working (*theo* + *urg*). More specifically, the oldest preserved theurgic teachings of the Sacred Way Home (see the chart, fig. 1)—those of ancient Egypt and China—tell of a goddess-inspired, transcendent "pregnancy." One that takes place within our still mysterious brain and body (of either sex)[1] leading to the attainment, even during lifetime on earth, of a higher body concealed until the physical death of the former one and far more endowed with energy and capability than the biomolecular body in which it forms, as within a womb or a chrysalid or pupal shell, symbolized in ancient Egypt as the enswathed mummy in its case.

It is an embryology of metamorphosis that is here involved, stemming from the premise that we are larval forms—a premise very startling to a largely agnostic and indeed rather ignorant culture, knowledgeable really only in the technology of external manipulations upon matter. We know next to nothing of how living bodies organize themselves from within and have their ultimate controls in regions of more than what ordinary quinto-sensory awareness is capable of grasping.

SOME BAD NEWS

The current global technological civilization is increasingly show-ing itself to be inimical to all life-forms except perhaps the most hardy of sewer and wharf rats, other assorted parasites, and those few bacterial prodigies that can survive even in highly radioactive waste. Yet aside from its biophobic or life-destroying aspect, the prevalent world society is the first widespread culture in history to be committed to conditioning its members to accepting—without any rational basis, much less evidence—that there is (1) no scheme of things other than the molecular one in which we live on earth, and (2) no higher than human intelligence and ability, and hence (3) that individualized personality and living form cease with the physical dissolution of the molecular body. These unproven and, in fact, quite scientifically dubious dogmas are then made the basis of our educational system, leading at once to both a jungle-law society and, in other aspects, to an essentially hopeless and com-fortless collectivism which ultimately reduces all individual suffer-ing and learning to meaninglessness.

Since only love in some form gives meaning to life, the power of love is also finally denied in the shabby and shoddy creed of hopelessness being foisted upon us by patterns of paranoid power-seeking that, by and large, tend to seize control of world society in the dark ages of the latter twentieth century. It is no accident that, contrasted with a 2½ percent rise of general suicide in the United States over the last decade, there was a 44 percent rise in the suicide rate for the age group of fourteen to nineteen-year-olds, about eighteen times as many: our children are being systematically deprived of hope by a system fast losing the perennial ideals.

The voices of the comparatively few leaders of integrity left are voices mostly crying in a growing wilderness of poisoned ecology and psychopathological social systems motivated by tyranny or short-term greed and the increasing fear, panic, and aggression that inevitably accompany such a degraded set of values. To cite one of these voices: "There is a very real possibility that man—through ignorance or indifference or both—is irreversibly altering the ability of our atmosphere to support life." These are not the words of some minor prophet of doom, but the sober, considered conclusions of the chairman of the U.S. congressional committee on the environment, reporting in June 1986 and cited in *Newsweek* magazine.

THE GOOD NEWS

But most of us now no longer need to be convinced of these trends. We are aware of them only too acutely. We don't need to hear any more bad news. We do want to hear about hope and where we can look for it. This chapter is concerned with that hope. As Joseph Conrad once wrote, the last hope of mankind will contain some almost unimaginably good news, though based on ideas well-nigh unutterable in terms of ordinary ways of thinking.[2]

That hope stretches far back in recorded history and concerns what may be called higher transformation. In brief, the present life-forms, and notably human beings, must be regarded as *larval forms* whose destiny it is to transform themselves into higher ones capable of living under very different conditions and of exercising powers which would seem quite extraordinary to us in our present state. That is the message of the "Crucible" (fig. 1).

Anyone who has ever raised caterpillars of, say, the lovely giant moths like Io, Cecropia, Luna, or Prometheus knows that the caterpillar does not at all fear its ineluctable metamorphosis, when the larva sheds its skin and becomes the quasi-entombed, cocooned pupal form deprived of almost all exterior mobility except to twist and turn its abdomen. So when author Richard Bach wrote that the caterpillar looks on its pupation as "death," he wrote too superficially, without having well observed a forming or hatching chrysalis.

The truth is far more interesting. The caterpillar shows by all its behavior, so intense at the cocoon-spinning or chrysalis-forming time, that its entire being is focused and intent upon this

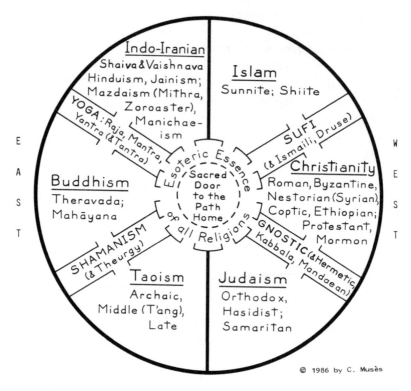

The Crucible of World Religions and Their Convergence on the Way Home: Distillation of the Essential Central Sacredness.

FIG. 1. *The Crucible of World Religions and Their Convergence on the Way Home: Distillation of the Essential Central Sacredness.* This mandalic-maze-circuit diagram is well-nigh self-explanatory—designed to show in one view the interrelations of the search for the Divine through the religions of human history, both in their institutionalized and more esoteric forms.

Depending on one's inherited cultural background and individual tendencies—and the two might not be in phase—one follows a path in the crucible. For some, whole lifetimes could be spent just on the fringes of the wheel. Others reach one of the spokes. Some again may even gain access to the first central area in which the particular cultural origin of a religion becomes irrelevant in that numinous nimbus. Beyond the door within that nimbus is the meaning of the whole crucible and its gestational process: the essential distillation at its core, where one begins to undertake the far journey home—the Lion Path in ancient Egypt.

The preparation and technique for that path, which transforms one as one treads it, exist in fragmentary form in the old human records. But those instructions, that operational method, are always available in great clarity to those who again reach that place of accessibility in awareness. Then one can start the heroic quest described in these lines from an obscure poet, Kyril Demys, three decades ago (who also wrote "Song of the Far Journey").

> *The doors are many*
> *but the key is one . . .*
> *that space has room*
>
> *for a winged and wondrous child*
> *and whirled a little world to being. . . .*
> *That child alone*
> *shall fly the abyss*
> *and reach the Second Sun.*

change—life itself for the caterpillar and not death at all. From a ravenous and mobile feeder, it now becomes very quiet, fasting and renouncing all food. Then it commences a new and excited round of activity in weaving its cocoon around itself, ending with a hard-varnished core-shell in which it leaves an almost imperceptible air pore. Here it finally discards its caterpillar skin, and the pupal case with wings, tongue, and antennae outlined on it appears.

Although there is no outer activity, there is now intense activity *within* the pupa, called a chrysalis in the case of butterflies because of its often golden (Greek *chrysos,* "gold") appearance. Inside the pupal form, all the caterpillar's internal organs now become transformed. Reproductive organs and new digestive organs are formed, as well as new organs of locomotion, notably two pairs of gorgeously colored wings. Note well that there is an *increase* and not a decrease of individuation in this process, and each winged adult is a specifically individual creature of distinct color, pattern, and sex. The *imago,* as it is called, is more, not less, individually organically differentiated than the caterpillar. So this metamorphic transformation, an actually higher embryology, leads to both greater powers (for example, of sexuality and flight) and to greater individualization.

THE SECRET WITHIN THE BRAIN

The caterpillar is so intensely active about ensuring its own disappearance for the very good reason that it innately realizes it is preparing a greater and richer life for itself, made possible through a group of neurosecretory glands connected with the caterpillar's central ganglion or tiny brain. This new life is an individual *outcome* for each caterpillar—the very opposite of merging into some engulfing collectivity. Tomb-transcending is nothing if not individual, and as I once wrote of tathagatahood in Mahāyana Buddhism: "Salvation, though it have universal results, has by necessity particular achievement."[3]

Similarly, the ancient theurgic doctrine taught that in the dim and mysterious recesses of each human brain are lodged the control centers for transducing a higher metamorphic process in that individual, of which the butterfly, wonderful as it is, is but a crude and imperfect analogue. Those who do not come to activate this process during their physical lifetimes have no choice but to enter the postmortem or interincarnational state as the "caterpillars" they were here. That state is called the *Duat* in ancient Egyptian, corresponding to the *Bardo* of Tibetan shamanistic Buddhism and the intermediate states of ancient Chinese shamanism that came to be Taoism. For those who did not begin the metamorphic process before dissolution of their physical bodies, this intermediate state would be dreamlike: lovely or nightmarish depending on the person's development and stature as a human being.

But if the transformational process were initiated *before* molecular dissolution, then the intermediate state could continue the process and the "hatching" might take place in the *Duat* or *Bardo* state, thus avoiding the necessity for further entries of the individual into relatively crude molecular bodies such as we on earth have, wonderful as they are for this stage. The acquisition of a higher body by an individual meant also, by that very token, the possibility of communicating with beings already so endowed.[4] The entrance into this higher community and fellowship is one of the principal causes for celebration in the Ancient Egyptian liturgy of the sacred transformative process—sacred because it conferred so much beyond ordinary ken.[5]

HIGHER RITES OF PASSAGE

On folio 237 of the great *Codex Manesso* (dated about 1425) now at the university library of Heidelberg, there is a magnificent depiction of Liechtenstein's renowned thirteenth-century troubadour Ulrich bearing on his helmet an image of the Goddess in her form of *Minne,* who presided over chivalric love. Her name has a fascinating etymology, linked to the Indo-European root *men-* (English, "mind") as the seat of consciousness—the same that the Ancient Egyptian and Old Chinese called "the heart." Her form, preserved by Ulrich's late medieval chronicler, wields a down-pointing arrow in the right hand, and the left arm holds aloft a flaming torch,[6] for she is Mistress of both death and life in that order. She is Mut, Great Mother of Death, and also Isis/Sothis, whose love makes possible the higher birth of Horus from the inert Osiris. As Ta-Urt, ruling the Great Dipper (in Egyptian called "the skin of Set" or the physical body destined for dissolution), she governs the dismemberment and recycling of that temporary vehicle until enough experience has been garnered to go on to a nondeath-interrupted mode of life. This is the deep reason why all great love, from Tristan and Iseut (= Isolde) to the Central Asiatic Na-Khi love-death pacts reported by botanist-ethnographer Joseph F Rock, is so deeply linked to death as a rite of passage.

In the old Celtic traditions preserved in the early Breton/ Gaulish romances of the twelfth century, love characteristically triumphed through death itself.[7] The Goddess was always there, as that prince of troubadours, Dante Alighieri,[8] depicted in his too-soon departed and beloved Beatrice, who became his divine protectress during the cosmic shamanic journey he unforgettably describes in *La Divina Commedia,* culminating in her Universal Love: "But yet the Will rolls onward like a wheel in even motion, by the Love impelled that moves the Sun in heaven and all the Stars." The goal in this life was to balance heaven and earth (incidentally, a very Chinese function for man). As the Swabian troubadour Meister Vridank (fl. 1200) wrote in his *Instruction in Discrimination (Bescheidenheit),* "Who God and World can encompass, there is a blessed one indeed." In profound ways the society of the twelfth and thirteenth centuries was the pinnacle of Western civilization, teaching, as it did, an apotheosis through love.

The present society, however,—forcing people more and more to think only of physical survival and material support,—naturally tends to block the perception of suprabiological fact and our participation in such a higher process. There is then the sheer dulling effect of leaving no time for such considerations in a person's daily life, whereas in the anciently taught theurgic societies such truths and participation in them were the central core and point of human life. The blocking tendency must be combated.

It is simply not true that our higher heritage will be just as active if we concern ourselves with our material existence alone. On the contrary, it will not be activated unless concern with it reflects consistently in a corresponding self-attunement with it in our *behavior.* Our actual creed is inescapably made manifest in how we behave, regardless of what anyone may verbally profess.

THE PRICE AND THE PROCESS

So the principal price to be paid for development leading to a higher body and life is the price every imminently pupating caterpillar pays: principal and regular dedication to that process and project. But if a caterpillar's metamorphic glands are tied off or blocked, it will simply live out its life as a caterpillar and never change. Thus, many human beings will not choose to activate themselves transformationally. But those who do and will, will inspire and help the rest, just as even our material, technological civilization rests upon the inventions, dedication, and genius of a comparative handful. The average *Bardo* experience is passionate and dreamlike, releasing the full force of a Freudian type of unconscious. In fact, never having read Sophocles' *Oedipus Rex* or *Electra* and also incredibly anticipating Freud, the great Tibetan commentator Drashi Namjal wrote that one who will be born as a man already begins in the *Bardo* realm to hate his future father and love his mother;[9] *mutatis mutandi* for one who will be born a woman.[10] The powerful unconscious drives released with full impact in the *Bardo* must sooner or later be dealt with and sublimed, there or here (in the alchemical sense).

In *The Lion Path,*[11] to which the reader is referred for more details, you will find the basis of the ancient Egyptian method. And in the forthcoming *Way of the Tiger (Hu[3] Tao[4]*—see fig. 2),[12] its Chinese counterpart will be described. Suffice it to say here, just as in Egypt, the ultimate basis for the method is based on the feminine aspect of divinity. Indeed, the earliest theurgic practitioner in China was not the shaman but the shamaness,[13] and the

Hu³	TIGER
Tao⁴	WAY
Shih⁴	IS (PRECISELY)
Tzu³	YOUR
Yüan²	ORIGIN(AL STATE)
Yu²	RETURN (JOURNEY)

The Way of the Tiger.

FIG. 2. *The Way of the Tiger.* This arcane Taoist sentence reads Hu^3 Tao^4 $shih^4$ tzu^3 $yüan^2$ yu^2: "The Way of the Tiger is nothing but your journey to your original state." What we are here being taught is that humanity's prime problem is not how to "progress" but rather how to *regenerate* (re-grow), recover, restore, and re-find in us what had been grossly overlaid but now refound refined.

The word for *journey* here is the verb yu^2, which originally meant "to swim," as across a river. Thus, journeying across the great stream of time and death into a region of harmony ($ch'i^2$: see fig. 2) was depicted by *I Ching* hexagram 63 Chi^4 Chi^4, the meaning and radical of the second "chi^4" which is deeply related to the last character (yu^2) of this sentence. As before noted the ordinary (Confucian) interpretation of hexagram 63 is misled and misleading. The key hexagram is 63, expressing the secret of the *Book of Changes,* and hexagram 64 ("Before the Crossing") expresses simply an anticlimactic recycling for those who did not complete the Heroic Journey of hexagram 63.

very character *wu*[1] ⫯ for shamanic theurgy includes two ritually dancing priestesses, *ƒ* and *ʎ* in the seal characters, doing the work *kung*[1] ⊥ of summoning divine powers.

Much of this process had to do with perceiving higher light associated with certain stars,[14] in particular with the seven stars of the Northern Dipper, named similarly in Chinese, and their two hidden celestial control centers, making nine in all—the same sacred number as in ancient Egypt, where Sothis-Isis (in hippopotamus form) and Osiris-Horus (in spear-thrower form) controlled the seven stars of the *Meskhent* or "birth tent" symbolizing the cast-off "skin of Set"[15] (i.e., the earthly body, that *Meskhent* or bull-skin being the constellational image of the seven principal Dipper stars in ancient Egypt). The Chinese doctrine again reflects Egypt.

The Chinese version involves also the magic Pace of Yü, legendary ruler and spiritual teacher who mastered the use of the celestial powers for the benefit of mankind and taught how to realize an immortal body no longer subject to molecular dissolution. The Pace of Yü was still performed by female shamans in South China as late as the 1960s.[16]

How the ritual nine-steps Pace of Yü was related to the *I Ching,* and specifically to the nine marks of hexagram number 63 (see fig. 3), we have explained in a paper presented to the American Oriental Society in 1986, and it need not detain us here. Also, it will appear in *The Way of the Tiger.*

THE PACE OF YU AND HEXAGRAM NO. 63: ULTIMATE SECRET OF THE I CHING

In the *Nei P'ien* of Ko Hung (fl. 320),[17] we read (chap. 17, p. 5 recto, col. 3) an ancient tradition recorded by that remarkable compiler:

> As you perform the Pace of Yü you will keep forming hexagram number 63:
>> First one foot forward
>> from an initial two side by side,

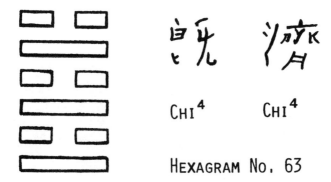

CHI⁴   CHI⁴

HEXAGRAM No. 63

FIG. 3. *I Ching Hexagram Number 63.* It is named *Chi⁴ Chi⁴* (two quite different characters of same sound and tone) and means "after being fulfilled or aided"; literally, "reaching the harmony (the character *ch'i²* embedded in the second *chi⁴*) of the other shore after having crossed over the river." Its empty translation as "after completion" is misleading if not erroneous. The nine marks or "footprints" of this hexagram are linked in esoteric Taoist tradition with the ninefold pace of the eponymous *Yü³,* the ancient demigod ruler of China ("Yü the Great" is the legendary founder of the First, or *Hsia⁴,* Dynasty), who had been taught by a master of "Bell Mountain" (*Chung¹ Shan¹*). Learning and following the Pace of Yü brought the adept starry rescue and power, and its nine steps (allied to the 7 + 2 Dipper stars) are also the nine cauldrons of transformation, in each of which Yü brewed an essential ingredient of the elixir of immortality. They are also his "nine numinous jewels" of the crown of mastery of life, essences distilled from the cauldrons.

The difference between this hexagram and number 64 ("Before crossing over or fulfillment") is that the lines (yang or yin) agree with their places (odd or even), whereas in number 64 they are completely out of harmony with their places. Thus, if we try to surpass the Pace of Yü, we find ourselves recycled and back at square one of the game board and must begin over again. The conventional Confucian interpretation (spread predominantly throughout the West) of this profound and key hexagram is in serious error. But the *I Ching* is essentially Taoist, and it is in the recondite reaches of Taoist teaching that we learn the *Book of Changes.*

143

These, though, do not suffice,
for nine prints are needed,
treaded in sequence to the end.

Three steps (three marks per step) yield 21 feet since one pace or step traverses 7 feet. On looking back you will see nine marks (footprints). [See fig. 4.]

Method for treading the Pace of Yü: (From an initial position with the two feet side by side) advance the right foot while left remains still. Then advance in sequence left and then right foot bringing it up to be side by side with left so that they are again side by side. This is step No. 1.

Now advance first right and then left foot and then bring up the right foot to be side by side with left. That is step No. 2. Now advance the left and then the right foot, and bring up the left to be side by side with the right. This is step No. 3, which completes a single Pace of Yü. It should be known to all who practice spiritual alchemy.

The rule for step number 1 practice is obviously corrupted here, since the successive steps should start not with the same but with alternating left and right feet to agree with yin/yang Taoist doctrine. But chapter 11, page 16 verso, restores the text and adds even more information:

> The Pace of Yü: Advance first left foot, then surpass its distance with an advancing right foot, and finally bring up left to right foot, then advance the right foot, pass it with the left, and bring up right to be side by side with left foot. Then advance left foot as at the start. In these 3 steps you will have traversed 21 foot-lengths and 9 prints will thus be made.

The two descriptions of the Pace of Yü thus give (1) right foot first, (2) right first again, (3) left foot first; and (1) left foot first, (2) right foot first, (3) left foot first.

Clearly, the alternation of the second description is in accord with Taoist axioms while step 1 of the first is not; so we see the partially corrupted passage of Ko's chapter 17, page 5 recto, is to be restored by his passage of chapter 11, page 16 recto. Neither passage has been hitherto noticed.

The relation to hexagram 63 is clear if we realize the code: that the movement bringing the two feet together constitutes a joining, designated by an unbroken line or yang stroke; while the motion of two steps formed by the feet being separated by different directions is designated by a broken line or yin stroke. Then, as one looks back at the nine footprints, the lines of hexagram 63 in order (the bottom line of a hexagram being line 1 and the top one line 6) can be seen in order as (1) —; (2) ––; (3) —; (4) ––; (5) —; and (6) ––; which we may translate thus into terms of the Pace of Yü (see fig. 4):

Step 1: From a position of the two feet together (—), advance the left foot curvingly to left and then advance right foot beyond it and forward (––), finally bringing up the left foot to it.

Step 2. From this new, realigned position (—), now advance the right foot curvingly to the right, then the left foot beyond it and forward (––), finally bringing up the right foot to where the left is.

Step 3: From this newly aligned position (—), repeat step 1.

Thus we have the nine "prints" spoken of in the mnemonic verse encoded as a sequence of the 9 marks —, ––, —, ––, —, –– comprising hexagram 63 with all its lines in agreeing, self-reinforcing places like a laser's coherent light beam.

There are two further considerations here: the key to the *I Ching* and the relation of this key to sacred stars and their powers or synchronous influences.

First, the entire pattern (and still mysterious) sequence of hexa-grams from number 1 ☰☰ and its paired number 2 ☷☷ to number 63 ䷾ and its paired number 64 ䷿ repre-sents a procession from separation of yang (—) and yin (––) lines to their mixing, which is self-annulling in number 64, since yin lines are on yang places and vice versa, like two waves of light

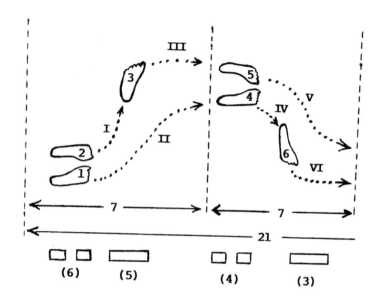

FIG. 4. *The Pace of Yü.* Making hexagram 63, you will have taken 9 steps (Roman numerals) or 3 paces of 7 footlengths each and covered 21 footlengths, leaving 9 footprints (Arabic numerals). The

mutually cancelling because of their 180° phase difference. The entire process is not static but subtle, dynamic, and ongoing, with a trap or reversal at number 64 if we try to push beyond the full appropriateness of number 63. Thus, hexagram 64 with its theme of retardation in development ("not yet swum across the [time] stream to the harmonious fields") is postclimactic and denotes not a fulfillment but instead an impending recycling or reversion—a going-back-to-square-one, so to speak. Hexagram number 64 (*Wei⁴ Ch'i²*) is *not* the culmination of the I Ching but an anticlimax.

Like all texts of any ancient language, the I Ching has not fared too well in translation, and confusions and superficialities tend to be perpetuated by too uninformed popularizers anxious to ride the I Ching bandwagon of growing popularity. Moreover, the Confucian school commentary at worst becomes banal and a rather

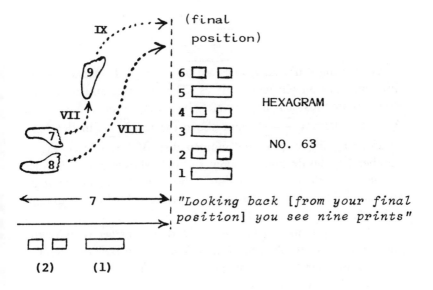

numbers in parentheses refer to the similarly numbered lines of hexagram 63 on the right. (Drawing not to scale.)

lifeless equilibrium without development, newness, or point—actually calling for a big "So what?" Thus, hexagram number 64 is mostly seen translated as "Before completion," whereas it actually means "(the state of) not yet having attained harmony," a richer, much more specific concept. Indeed, the *wei⁴* character also corresponds to the eighth "branch" among the cyclical twelve: the Chinese version of the sign Scorpio, in turn, classically corresponding to death, disintegration, and consequent recycling—the result of not yet having "swum the stream" (i.e., achieved the profound harmony of one's nature with the cosmos leading to regeneration, apotheosis, and the entrance into a higher community of more advanced evolutionary stage than we—a stage possessing a body not subject to mortal conditions). The Taoists called such suprahuman beings *hsien¹:* "transcendent immortals."

147

The real climax and culmination of the *I Ching* occurs at the sixty-third hexagram: *Chi⁴ Ch'i²* or "the Achievement of Harmony" and its line pattern is 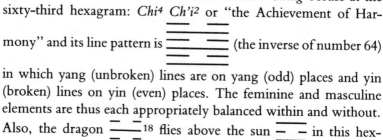 (the inverse of number 64) in which yang (unbroken) lines are on yang (odd) places and yin (broken) lines on yin (even) places. The feminine and masculine elements are thus each appropriately balanced within and without. Also, the dragon ——[18] flies above the sun — — in this hexagram, carrying it as in the winged disk of Egypt; whereas in number 64, the dragon is below the sun, showing a basic misjoinder, since the dragon's region is the invisible highest heavens, and the visible, fiery jewel is meant to be carried below the dragon in its claws.

The analysis ineluctably leads us to the answer to why the ancient tradition ascribed the Pace of Yü, who walked through the stars to immortality, to the pattern of *Chi⁴ Ch'i²,* hexagram number 63, as the *Nei P'ien* clearly states.

The three like pairs (———) of lines are the three steps that together form the Pace of Yü, comprised of "nine marks," there being nine strokes to the hexagram (as there are in number 64, but there each line is on an inharmonious place for itself; whereas in number 63 the nature of the lines and the places agree and harmonize).

We can also regard this hexagram as a choreographic encoding of the dance of Yü as shown in fig. 4. Each unbroken (or yang) line represents the two feet come together, whereas the broken (or yin) lines show the feet separated by different motions. Thus, the first pair of lines of hexagram number 63 shows that, from the initial together position, one foot (the left, as the ancient tradition recorded by Ko Hung tells us) is advanced in a wavelike path, and then the other, in movements reminiscent of the traditional *T'ai Chi Ch'üan* practice.

If we fulfill the indicated choreography, we must perform the threefold pace constituting a march of Yü. So not only does each pace or step have nine characteristic code marks, but the unit march of Yü described in the ancient tradition consists of three paces or 9 movements, as we have seen. Hexagram number 63 thus represents the choreography of Yü on his path to a dynamic immortality, to the Ever-Blossoming State, the never-dead condition, the ever-living one.

We can now map the completed Pace of Yü in three times 9 steps thus, the five rising or male nodes shown by rising arrows and the four falling or female nodes by descending arrows, in fig. 5.

A different and later scheme by Yüan Miao-tsung (fl. twelfth

century) reproduced in Schafer[19]

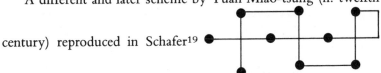

(each of the nine points here representing a pair of footprints in the clearly corrupted diagram with impossible indications of direction) does not fit the ancient criteria. For instance, in no event would it accomplish the traversal of the thrice seven-foot lengths called for, nor could hexagram number 63 choreograph it.

We are now ready for a second consideration—one of astral affinities. In chapter 15, page 11 verso, column 2, of the *Nei P'ien,*[20] the practitioner of the Pace of Yü is related to the seven stars of the Northern Dipper and in one practice imagines its bowl over his head and its "handle" pointing at whatever danger confronts.

From fig. 5 we see that the full Pace of Yü traces out a set of 4 + 5 = 9 nodes: ₀°₀°₀°₀°₀. In the author's collection is a ritual jade "star sword" with the seven sacred dipper stars marked out thus: •••• and, as Edward H. Schafer has made clear in his useful treatise *Pacing the Void,* there was an important tradition of nine and not only seven sacred stars, the eighth and ninth being invisible and called "the Rescuer-Protector"[21] and "the Sustainer." Confirming our opening quotation from Ko Hung (which he missed), Schafer, however, demonstrated that the Pace of Yü is traditionally linked with these nine sacred stars. The sevenfold scheme is thus enlarged to •••••, agreeing with fig. 5 and the ancient prescription for the Pace of Yü reported by Ko Hung in his *Nei P'ien,* above cited.

149

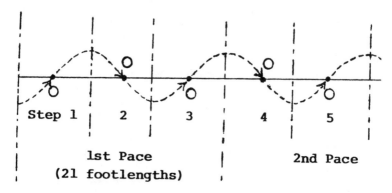

Step 1   2   3   4   5

1st Pace   2nd Pace
(21 footlengths)

FIG. 5. *One makes three times the Pace of Yü* with 9 steps in each Pace, thus answering to the 9 stages of each of the 3 High Realms, one traversed in each such pace of 9 steps, significantly making a total of 63 footlengths, again the number of the key hexagram (see figs. 3 and 4). One thus creates 9 nodes (the black dots on the wave), 5 ascending nodes (denoted by upward-pointing arrows), and 4 descending (denoted by downward-pointing arrows). These respectively correspond to the 5 male and the 4 female divinities presiding

We have now established that the full set of nine is referred to in the Pace of Yü and that consequently the Rescuer and Sustainer are ancient traditions and that also we naturally arrive at a male/female positioning of the nine, corresponding to the traditional Taoist transcendent group of five male and four female divinities and their palaces (microcosmically located at centers within the brain) as, for instance, in an esoteric Taoist work[22] of which Professor Edward Schafer first made me aware and kindly furnished photostats.[23]

The demonstration of the connection of the Pace of Yü with specific Taoist astrotheurgy and with the secret, central message of the *I Ching* itself is now completed.

Though Ho Kung or Pao-p'u tzu ("the Simpleton"—his self-adopted, ironic sobriquet) has often been misclassified as a Confucianist, he was always *au fond* Taoist, and he notes in his *Wai p'ien* that his work *Nei p'ien* is completely and definitely Taoist, which the text amply confirms. But his heart was, above all, with the Tao, and he eloquently wrote, during a strongly Confucian epoch,

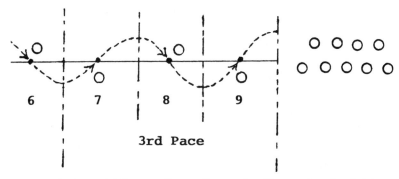

3rd Pace

over the 9 cranial "grottos" according to the diagram (on the right) of 5+4 small circles found in Taoist esoteric works such as the *shang⁴ ch'ing¹ ta⁴ tung⁴ chiu³ kung¹ chao¹ hsiu¹ pi⁴ chüeh² shang⁴ tao⁴* (mentioned in the section on Taoist sources), where it appears on the first page. These 9 regions and their powers also correspond to the 9 sacred stars. See too fig. 6 and the text around it, including the note on the "All-powerful Goddess."

in his autobiography, "My spirit was out of tune with my times. . . . I walked consistently against the direction of the masses."[24]

Pertinent here also are the nine cranial palaces or regions within the brain devoted to the seven-plus-two principal powers. There are several little-known Taoist treatises describing them.[25] More details will be given in *Way of the Tiger (Hu³ Tao⁴)*, but the point is that four of those key regions are ruled by female powers, including the principal seat of the higher transformation governed by the All-powerful Goddess[26] whose title was that of Isis: "Mother of the Crown Prince and Heir" (i.e., Mother of Horus, heir [and self-transform] of Osiris whose fourteenfold severed body symbolized the "fall" from a higher energy-substance into piecemeal molecular matter).

It remains to be said only that the Goddess's highest function was to promote a supernal pregnancy and ultimate birth carrying us beyond molecular dissolution or death and moreover carrying

151

FIG. 6. *The Nine Dipper Stars among the Na-khi of Western China.* The Nah-khi women (recalling the Chinese *wu¹* tradition of women being the original bearers of shamanic lore) wear on the backs of their sheepskin jackets symbols of the ancient doctrine of the 9 stars: 7, plus 2 rulers of great power. They wore these latter as 2 larger disks (which they said represented "a sun" and "a moon") on the back of each shoulder and, between these, 7 small disks for the 7 stars of the Dipper. As a group, these 9 disks were called (using Rock's tonal numbers and transcription, *A Na-Khi–English Encyclopedic Dictionary*) ³ma-²yü-³bpa, the 3 words literally meaning "disks in back / divine primal beings / dipper," the Na-khi using the same constellational image as the Chinese and ourselves for these stars.

us into a creative and beautiful fellowship with other similarly equipped and evolved beings—a plan as explicit as it is inspiring.

CONCLUSION/NEW BEGINNING

Against such a specific and suprabiological backdrop, arid verbalizings of some egghead Buddhists and Advaita Vedantists seem puerile exercises in rather pointless intellectualism. There is an apt seventeenth-century Taoist commentary found in Yang Chi-chou's great compilation, *Chen-chiu Ta-ch'eng*, republished at Peking (Beijing) in 1973: "Alas, the Buddhists do not understand the subtle energy channels in the body. They practice fasting, silence, cutting off their arms [as did the second Zen patriarch to show his piety], burn their bodies, stay seated and dry out. How sad!" For a commentary and French translation of part of his work, see Catherine Despeux's edition of the nineteenth-century Taoist teacher Chao Pi-ch'en (b. 1860).[27]

We also must not stop short, as Mircea Eliade and Carl Jung tend to do, in merely patronizing the old shamans while still denying the *ontological* validity of their claims, as though the whole subject were susceptible of being psychologized or anthropologized away. Rather must we undertake a supershamanic enterprise, that Heroic Journey[28] described so eloquently by Joseph Campbell,[29] knowing the instrumentalities for it can be forged within us by paying careful attention to what the Old Ones taught; for the nature of life and of our universe goes back to profoundly natural powers and wisdom we cannot even yet begin to conceive. The arrogant myth that "modern science" can "conquer nature" is mere hubris and, like all false pride, is very weak when the chips are down, as they are today.

In the closing days of a long cosmic cycle, we can gird up our loins and walk the lion path and the way of the tiger—walk to our natural and quite glorious destiny and heritage. Then nature will no longer be at war with humanity, as it is now because of human insult and injury upon her. But nature will then join hands with humanity as a friend and most powerful of magical allies. Our destiny is not to impose our dangerously limited intelligence upon all other living beings and ecological components but rather to walk with all of them into the dawn of a higher day—that "Coming Forth into Day" which was envisioned millennia ago on the banks of the Nile.

There is an almost clairvoyant intuitive testimony to the foregoing, one we found only shortly before this chapter was finished. It consists of less than five hundred words from early (1971) Doris Lessing, treating of a theme she never resumed and with an inspiration never surpassed.[30] Those who read *The Lion Path* concerning the sacred way home, written well before knowing of this passage of extracts from *Briefing for a Descent into Hell*, will be as interestingly surprised as we were.

Earth is due to receive a new pattern of impulses. The First Class Emergency Conference was convened on Venus and had delegates from as far away as Pluto. . . .

But the element in which this process exists is—Time. *Time is the whole point.* Timing. The surfer on the wave.

The life of humanity is governed elsewhere . . . was set by Mercury and Venus, Mars and Jupiter, Saturn, Neptune, Uranus, and Pluto. . . . This particular configuration of planets will really be so powerful—the equivalent of several centuries of evolution all in a decade or so. . . . But I expect there'll be the usual few who will listen. It's enough. . . .

Well, whatever stark and dire nature of the shortly-to-be-expected celestial configurations, and whatever man's backslidings, there is confidence in the outcome. . . . And if worse comes to worst, the Celestial Gardener will simply have to lop off that branch, and graft another.

People don't know it but it is as if they are living in poisoned air. They are not awake. They've been knocked on the head, long ago, and they don't know that is why they are living like zombies and killing each other. They know they should be doing something else, not just living hand to mouth, putting paint on their faces and decorating their caves and playing nasty tricks on their rivals.

But how can we be different? How can we get out? If you find out, will you come and take me with you?

It's all timing, you see. Sometimes it is easier for us to get out than other times.

There are people in the world all the time who know, but they are quiet. They just move about quietly, saving the people who know they are in the trap. And then, for the ones who have got out, it's like coming around from chloroform. They realise that all their lives they've been asleep and dreaming. And then it's their turn to learn the rules and the timing. And they become the ones who live quietly in the world. . . .

When the time comes, it will be our task to wake up those of us who have forgotten as well as to recruit suitable inhabitants of Earth—those, that is, who have kept a potential for evolving into rational beings; and to generally strengthen and defend our colonies on Earth for their task. That has always been so, of course, but this time it will be all that and more—it will be an assisting of the Earth's people through the coming Planetary Emergency.

It is significant that this explicit prophecy of divine transformation came through a woman. The Goddess still speaks. . . .

Indeed, as the following anecdote tells.

The late twentieth century may well go down as one of the darkest ages of human history. Yet, just as the blackest shadows are cast by the brightest of lights, so, along with all the terrible evils of environmental pollution, deep mental and emotional confusion, fruitless hatred, and lack of perception of anything higher than the merely human—along with all that, come the rays of highest inspiration, shed by the Lamp of Lamps for those to see who can. Those words were written in April 1986 across a continent and an ocean to a remarkable young woman, one of those rare persons seeking self-development at the expense of self-aggrandizement.

She replied that "it is because of the Infinite Mercy that at a time when the Truth is completely denied it is also opened in all its forms to those who still seek it. One could also say that this is a time when the most developed and highest evolved representatives from all religions can unite. I have personally noticed that there seems to be a sifting out of all those who adhere to the universal truth all over the world; they are being brought together or being put in touch with each other in the most incredible of ways. A network is being established from the briefest of encounters or the minimum of communication."

The reply, in part, was that what is now needed is no longer mere hand-wringing but a map and a method of walking to the Sanctuary and helping (and being helped by) those whose free decision is to walk there, too. "It is a high calling. But I believe nothing less would satisfy you."

Her next question was, "What makes you say that? I am sure you understand that I am asking not from idle curiosity."

The answer lies in the Path itself and those who desire it above all things. It is like the Sacred Floor, in the ancient hieroglyphic Book-of-the-Three-Ways, that asks, "Who tries to tread on me? Declare, if you can, my true name and nature, and your own intentions."

The Way is a living one, infinitely adaptable to individual natures but also infinitely discerning and discriminating in appraising those who profess to seek it. The opportunity is there for those with the self-dedication to perceive and pursue it. *Vámanos.*

THE TAOIST SOURCES

This section, principally addressed to those with some knowledge of or at least interest in the Chinese sources, concerns a briefly annotated selection of texts bearing importantly on ideas raised or discussed in this chapter. It also furnishes short indications of English, French, and German works containing translations, commentary, or further leads.

For the Chinese texts, we turn principally to that vast repository of the *Tao⁴ Tsang¹* or *Hoard of the Tao* (the Taoist prototype of the much later Tibetan *Tänjur* and *Känjur*). It will be abbreviated as TT and exists in a contemporary edition published at Shanghai in 1924–26. A branching compilation, the *Tao⁴ Tsang¹ Ching¹ Hau²,* or "The Cultivation of the Blossoms of the Tao Treasury," shall likewise be abbreviated TTCH. Tones are indicated by the usual superscripts in titles or phrases of special interest. For reasons of economy, the Chinese characters of titles are not printed here, but their TT and other references are sufficient, for those with enough knowledge to use them, to find them.

1. *Shang⁴ ch'ing¹ ta⁴ tung⁴ chiu³ kung¹ chao¹ hsiu¹ pi⁴ chüeh²
shang⁴ tao⁴* (TT 319), "The Dawn Practice of the Secret Teaching of the Supreme Way in the Nine Palaces of the Great Grotto of Superlative Clarity"; attributed to an otherwise unknown Chou Teh-ta as its transmitter from ancient times.

This text assigns both sun and moon ten rays each and makes the lunar image (yellow- or orange-rayed) one-ninth greater in diameter than the solar (complementarily purple-rayed). More importantly, it speaks of "a new-born child" within the cranial space of the aspirant, a divine babe embodying the power of the Lord of Immortality and who is named "germinal essence made visible." This whole idea is closely linked with the technical term "sacred pregnancy" (*sheng¹ t'ai¹*), esoterically synonymous with "jade pregnancy" (*yü⁴ t'ai¹*); that is, the nurture of an embryonic immortal being within one.

Many later teachers, for example, Yang Chi-chou, speak of this divine pregnancy that takes place within the aspirant, recalling that profound seer Jacob Böhme's inspired teaching that the Virgin Birth must take place within each of us if we are truly to become enlightened and "born again of the Spirit." It is interesting how little the fundamental parameters of a perennial teaching change.

2. *Shang⁴ ch'ing¹ ming² t'ang² yüan² chen¹ ching¹ chüeh²* (TT 194), "Scripture of Esoteric Teachings of the Primal Perfected Ones in the Luminous Chamber of Highest Clarity [i.e., the brain and its ventricles within the cranium]." The word *yüan²* ("primal") is given in the TT in the first mention of the title instead of *hsüan¹* ("hidden," "mysterious"), which is given in subsequent reference. But the two are not incompatible. This compilation contains as its principal treatise a work of singular import, the *Hsüan² chen¹ fa¹*, or "Method of the Mysterious Perfected Ones."

This text, we found, exists in two somewhat differing TT versions, one translated by Isabelle Robinet and the other by Edward Schafer a little later. For these references, see the second, or Western, section of this note.

This treatise may profitably be studied in conjunction with the *T'ao huang-ching: Teng-cheng yin-chüeh chen-ching* (TT 193).

3. *Shang⁴-ch'ing¹ ming²-t'ang² hsüan²-tan¹ chen¹-ching¹*, "The Scripture of Self-Perfecting by the Mysterious Elixir of the Bright Hall of the Realm of Highest Clarity" (TT 1043 = L. Wieger's designation 1362). This text contains a valuable description of the nine (4 goddess-governed + 5 god-ruled) cranial palaces, mentioned also in other texts and includes a conversation involving the T'ang dynasty Taoist teacher, Lü Tung-pin (in TT 641 = Wieger's no. 1005).

4. *Fei¹ hang² chiu³ chen¹ yü³ ching¹* (TT 195 and 1042), "The Scripture of the Nine Perfected Winged Ones Who Fly [through celestial realms]." In this compilation is found the important *Chiu³ hsing¹ tao⁴*, or "Way of the Nine Stars," that is to say, the Seven Dipper Stars and their two secret ruling stars (cf. fig. 4).

5. *Huang ch'i yang ching ching* (TT 27) and *Chin chou yü tsu* (TT 581); both these works date from well before A.D. 300 and are concerned with the practitioner's translation to the transcendent cosmic realm resonantly attuned to the stars of the Northern Dipper. It is worth noting that *t'ai²*, the word for the Great Dipper constellation, is also contained in the character of another *t'ai²*, meaning "embryo" or "pregnant womb." The Northern dipper was thus viewed as attuned to the process of higher pregnancy that eventuated in the divine embryo (*yü⁴ t'ai²*) of the immortal body.

Now we cite two works from the auxiliary Taoist treasury (TTCH).

6. *Ssu¹ hsiu¹ chiu³ kung¹ fa¹*, "*Method of Contemplative Practice on the Nine [Cranial] Palaces.*" TTCH, collection 7, book 4, is the *Yün² chi⁴ ch'i¹ ch'ien¹*, and the above-cited important treatise is its forty-third chapter. The entire work is listed immediately following.

7. *Yün² chi⁴ ch'i¹ ch'ien¹*, "The Cloud [i.e., celestial] Steps [as footprints on a path] of the Seven Symbols"—the seven refer to the cosmic powers assigned to the manifest Dipper Stars (TTCH, as

above cited, and also cf. TT 677–702, in the *Ssu pu ts'ung k'an* collection).

To those may be added the following.

8. *Chiu³ tz'u²* or "Nine Songs," basically invocatory poems of shamanesses of the old Ch'u kingdom (that in 750 B.C. was in the south in the Han and Yangtze valleys; then it spread north and eastward, annexing southern Kiangsu in the fourth century before our era). This work, admirably translated by Arthur Waley into English, dates as a compilation from ca. 350 B.C. and is part of the old shamanic anthology from Ch'u times, the *Ch'u tz'u*. Individual compositions in it are much older.

9. The *Nei⁴ P'ien¹* or "Inner (esoteric) Treatise" of Ko Hung (fl. A.D. 320). It still exists in the 1592 Chinese edition, and it was translated into English by James R. Ware.

We shall now, in the second part of this section, briefly give some indications of sources in Western languages. Some of these have already been mentioned at least in passing in the previous discussion of sources.

1. Isabelle Robinet, "Randonnées extatiques des Taoistes dans les astres," *Monumenta Serica* 32 (1976): 159–273. This is a valuable work and veritable mine of otherwise inaccessible translations and sources. She is a pioneer in this subject of theurgic journeys in Taoist tradition.

2. Edward H. Schafer, "The Jade Woman of Greatest Mystery," *History of Religions* 17 (1978): 393–96 especially. Another extremely valuable source for both subject material and further leads. In the meantime, Schafer's *Pacing the Void* appeared (University of California Press, Berkeley, 1977), a unique book also worthwhile consulting, to which can be added a masterly study.

3. Michael Strickmann, *Le taoïsme du Mao Chan; chronique d'une révélation.* (Paris: Institut des Hautes Études chinoises, 1980). And of course the path-breaking classical papers of Maspero published posthumously in

4. Henri Maspero, *Le taoïsme et les religions chinoises*, edited by Paul Demiéville (Paris: Gallimard, 1971).

5. Rolf Homann, *Die Wichtigste Körpergottheiten der Huang-t'ing ching*, Göppinger Akademische Beiträge Nr. 27 (Göppingen: Verlag Kümmerle, 1971). A pioneering and useful reference work containing some translation and more sources. Sometimes he is too literal and misses the esoteric terminology, thus translating *hsüan² tan¹* as *dunkler Zinnober* ("dark cinnabar") instead of "mysterious elixir"; but his book is very helpful.

6. Arthur Waley, *The Nine Songs*, (London: Allen & Unwin, 1965). An excellent annotated and commented translation. These shamanic songs had first been translated (into German) in Vienna in 1852 by August Pfizmaier in an extremely good rendition for its time. Nonsinologues still await a translation of the rest of the captivating *Ch'u tz'u*, the oldest extant shamanic anthology of China.

7. James R. Ware, *The Nei P'ien of Ko Hung* (Cambridge, MA: MIT Press, 1966). Ware is an excellent translator and furnishes an excellent Chinese glossary and useful discussion. He engagingly captures Ko Hung's loquacity and wit.

Finally, the writer is grateful to Isabelle Robinet, Edward Schafer, and Michel Strickmann for kindly providing time-saving guidance in the labyrinth of Taoist sources.

ADDENDUM

As this book was about to go to press, I came across a twelfth-century Taoist source authoritatively confirming a central conclusion of this chapter: that hexagram number 63 is the key to the deepest message of the *I Ching* and the doctrine underlying it. It is the work of Chang Po-Tuan (fl. 1250), one of the founders of the "Whole Reality" Taoist tradition, which played such an important role in the fourteenth-century edition of the *Dao Tsang*, the Taoist counterpart of the Tibetan *Känjur* and *Tänjur*.

In particular, in Chang's works *Comprehending Reality* and *Taoist Esoteric Doctrine* there are several passages showing that he regarded the trigrams Li (fire) and K'an (water) as referring to the conscious and unconscious mind, in turn. The former "flies up" and the latter "flows down," thus they must be reversed from their mutually separating configuration in hexagram 64. This inversion, then—shown in hexagram 63—is a symbol of the true alchemical process that must take place within the aspirant if she or he (the Taoists fully admitted female adepts) actually undertook the sacred inner development of the germ of the immortal body. The key importance of hexagram 63 to the solution of the enigma of the Pace of Yü and of the deepest meaning of Chinese alchemy is, of course, a central *leitmotif* of this chapter.

Notes

1. The caterpillar is latently already male or female, metamorphosing into the winged adult of its own, now manifest, sex.

2. "I am inclined to think that the last utterance [of humanity] will formulate some hope now to us utterly inconceivable." Joseph Conrad.

3. C. Musès, *Schopenhauer's Optimism and the Lankavatara Sutra* (London: Watkins, 1955).

4. A Gnostic inheritance from Egypt was the notion of a "body of light," the self-luminous vehicle called *augoeides*.

5. *The Lion Path* (obtainable through House of Horus, 45911 Silver Avenue, Sardis, British Columbia, V2R 1Y8, Canada) explains this process in more detail based on the hieroglyphic texts.

6. This ancient trait is preserved by the French sculptor Frédéric Bartholdi in the famous, recently rededicated American Statue of Liberty, first unveiled in October 1886 in New York harbor after having been offered to and refused by the British authorities of Suez.

7. Millennially antedating the Judeo-Christian veneer as the later attempts (for example, in the rambling Lancelot-Grail narrative) to christianize those ancient traditions prove. See Musès, "Celtic Origins and the Arthurian Cycle: Geographic-Linguistic Evidence," *Journal of Indo-European Studies* 7 (1979): 31–48; and also *Destiny and Control in Human Systems* (Boston and Dordrecht: Kluwer-Nijhoff, 1985), chap. 5.

8. See his *Canzoni*.

9. See his commentary-abridgment of Naropa's *Six Yogas*. The only available translation we know of Drashi's work is that of C. C. Chang (*Naropa's Six Yogas* [New Hyde Park, NY: University Books, 1963], 51ff.), who worked with the present writer on the book *Esoteric Teachings of the Tibetan Tantra*, 2d ed. (York Beach, ME: Weiser, 1982).

10. This sentence, no more than Freud's metaphoric processes, should not be taken too literally or applied too rigidly. It is not a universal problem. We are simply making the point here that the Freudians were well anticipated by early Tibetan psychologists.

11. Musaios, *The Lion Path* (Berkeley, CA: Golden Sceptre, 1989).

12. The superscript numbers (1, 2, 3, or 4), in the transliteration of Chinese words, denote tones by the usual convention.

13. I prefer this to Edward Schafer's more artificial and opaque *shamanka*.

14. Someone, with an air of pseudoprofundity, once wrote that we never see light but only see by light. Worse, that someone was solemnly quoted: blind leading the blind. The would-be sage had evidently seen only objects by reflected light and had never seen transmitted light. In fact, we see light all the time: the light of the stars is the only star we ever see—and sometimes that light is very old light at that—millennia old and more. We see nothing *but* the light from the stars. We must improve the quality of our intellectual light so that we are not subservient to superficial paradoxes. Enough said . . .

15. The *ínm-n-Stš* or "hide-of Set": *mes-n-Stš*.

16. W. Eberhard, *Local Cultures of South and East China* (Leiden: Brill, 1968), 74–75.

17. This is his "inner" or esoteric book, as contrasted with Ko Hung's *Wai P'ien,* the external or exoteric book. See our section on Taoist sources, part 2, item 7.

18. Compare this trigram's ancient form:

19. See our section on Taoist sources, second part, under item 2: *Pacing the Void,* p. 240.

20. See section on Taoist sources, part two, item 7.

21. We prefer this as a translation of the character whose etymology shows an imprisoned man being aided on either side by armed helpers.

22. Item 1 of the first part of the section on Taoist sources.

23. Personal communication of December 1, 1985.

24. Ware translates this lively and trenchant autobiography in style. See Taoist sources, part two, item 7, pp. 6–21.

25. See the later discussion of the Taoist sources.

26. Sometimes called Jade Lady of Greatest Mystery, the Chinese character for "jade" (*yü⁴*) here being a euphemism for "immortal" or a "mysterious perfected one" (*hsüan² chen¹*). Thus, in ancient Chinese formal burials, six ritual jades were placed around the body of the deceased in each of the cardinal directions as well as above and below (B. Lauffer, *Jade* [New York: Dover, 1974], 294–305, 120ff.). On one of these jades the seven (–cum-nine) stars were featured, the same that still survived until recent times as the nine symbolic ornaments (fig. 6) on the backs of women's garments (as in ancient China, the women carried on the shamanic tradition) among the *Na-khi,* a Sino-Tibetan people of far-West China (J. F. Rock, *A Na-Ki–English Encyclopedic Dictionary,*

part 1 [Rome: Istituto Italiano per il Medio ed Estremo Oriente, 1963]). See fig. 5 also.

27. Published by Les Deux Océans, Paris, 1979.

28. Musès, *Schopenhauer's Optimism,* 49.

29. In his *Hero with a Thousand Faces,* Bollingen Foundation, New York, 1949.

30. D. Lessing, *Briefing for a Descent into Hell* (New York: Alfred A. Knopf, 1971).

References

Musès, C., *Schopenhauer's Optimism and the Lankavatara Sutra,* Watkins, London, 1955.

Musès, C., "Celtic Origins and the Arthurian Cycle: Geographic-Linguistic Evidence" in *J. of Indo-European Studies,* vol. 7 (1979), pp. 31–48.

Musès, C., *Destiny and Control in Human Systems,* Kluwer-Nijhoff, Boston-Dordrecht, 1985.

Drashi, Namjal, *Naropa's Six Yogas* (tr. C.C. Chang), University Books, New Hyde Park, New York, 1963, pp. 51ff.

Musès, C., ed., *Esoteric Teachings of the Tibetan Tantra* (tr. C.C. Chang), 2nd. ed., Weiser, York Beach, Maine, 1982.

Musaios, *The Lion Path,* Golden Sceptre, Berkeley, California, 1989.

Eberhard, W., *Local Cultures of South and East China,* Brill, Leiden, 1968, pp. 74–75.

Laufer, B., *Jade,* Dover, New York, 1974, pp. 294–305 and 120ff.

Rock, J. F., *A Na-Khi—English Encyclopedic Dictionary* (Part I), Istituto Italiano per il Medio ed Estremo Oriente, Rome, 1963.

Lessing, D., *Briefing for a Descent into Hell,* Alfred A. Knopf, New York, 1971.

EPILOGUE
A Celebration of Goddess

*Nor can it be doubted that a cult of the One
Madonna existed already in the Paleolithic age.*
— Ananda Coomaraswamy,
The Ṛg Veda as Land-Náma-Bók, 1935

I. LALITĀSAHASRANĀMAM
(The Thousand Names of the Goddess)

Introduction to the Great Mother of the Universe:
The First Eighty-three Names
—AYESHAH HALEEM

Śrīmātā!—Glorious Mother!
Śrimāhārājnī!—Glorious Queen!
Śrimatsimhāsaneswarī!—Glorious Ruler on the Lioness Throne!

Thus begins, with her first three names, the uplifted Sanskrit hymn Lalitāsahasranāmam (The Thousand Names of the Goddess) in praise of the Goddess of our Universe, with forms of address describing her prime triplicity as Container, Measurer, and Matter of the Universe (all implied by the word *Mātā;*[1] Queen of the Universe thereby; and Regulator of Time, the Devouring Lioness)—and therefore of all cycles that eventually return to their starting point, making a whole.

Although her triple quality is all-encompassing, she is Manifestation itself (*Māyā*)—the Veil of Existence—in all its variety and detail, and thus she may be found through countless avenues. It is something of this multiplicity that *The Thousand Names of Lalitā* seeks to convey, though the "thousand," in turn, stand for the thousands upon thousands of epithets that actually exist. The

165

text now available,[2] although a compilation of recent date, is without doubt derived from prototypes reaching back several millennia before Christ and eventually to Paleolithic times.

It does not have a completely clear-cut structure, but within the morass of names, clusters group together in particular themes: the first eighty-three names—with which we are concerned here—primarily describe her manifest form and her martial prowess against evil of all kinds. Because the World is Form and she is the World, the hymn begins with a description of her shape in terms of the most beautiful female body conceivable, made all the more desirable by its vegetable and mineral accoutrements. Metaphysically, it is a presentation of the Way to Goddess via a goddess, whether in human or statue or icon form—a way accessible to human beings at any level of understanding, a beginning on physical and biological foundations which have to be seen as symbolic vehicles in order to lead to contact with the Goddess herself.

She is born in the sacred fire-vessel of Pure Intelligence (name 4) resplendent as a thousand rising suns (6), in order to perform the purpose of the Gods (5). Names 7–12 describe her in statue form, endowed with four arms that hold four weapons, the noose that lassos selfish desire; the elephant hook that controls anger; the sugar-cane bow of the flowing mind; and the arrows of the five elements, her radiance suffusing the entire Egg of Brahman with compassion. Many examples of Indian sculpture survive that embody these names and are still used as yantras.[3]

Names 13–51 lovingly enumerate her physical form: her hair gleams with sweetly smelling flowers and is caught up in a horned crest of rubies; her forehead is as beautiful as an expanse of the bright moon on the eighth day; her full-moon face is marked like an antelope is marked, with beauty spots; her eyebrows are . . . etc. This is the Goddess as Aphrodite, vehicle of physical beauty and bodily fulfilling love, the ground of Tantra.

Her supreme power is praised by Brahmā, Viṣṇu and Śiva (83), as well as by the ṛshis or seers (64). She sits on the fivefold seat of Brahmā (58); indeed, she is Śiva himself (53); and the lap of Śiva is also her throne (52). In an esoteric interpretation of name 71, the five angles of Śakti redeem the more static four angles of Śiva, their union creating the Śrīcakra.[4]

Other of the remaining names describe her centrality in Hindu terms: she dwells at the center of the peak of the heavenly Mount Meru (55); is leader of the Illustrious City therein (56); and dwells within the Wishing-Jewel House within that (57). Yet she is ubiquitous, residing also in the great thicket of Lotuses (59) or grove of kadamba trees (60). And the bliss experienced at reaching her is because she is established in the midst of the Ocean of Nectar (61).

But there is another side to her beauty which is the manifestation of her victorious energy, seen as Warrioress. Omitting a few, we now come to a cluster of very long names (65–82), each taking up a whole line of verse, which shows how the very illusions she has allowed to be created are routed and destroyed by her own *viaticum*,[5] since in the end all the powers of the universe are under her sway and can be used by her as her own armies. This is the Goddess as Athena/Minerva.

Earliest cult statues of Aphrodite show her armed (de Lasseur 1919) and accompanied by a lion (Hampe 1969, 35ff.). According to Simon (1969, 181f. and 231), Athena and Aphrodite were still closely related in Mycenaean times, as shown by the Arrephoros festival. Confirming this conclusion, on the akropolis of Gortin, Aphrodite and Athena were worshiped jointly (Rizza-Scrinari 1968).[6]

Thus, before Greek mythology in Mycenaean times separated Aphrodite from Athena, both aspects were seen as one goddess. The most enduring form of both in synthesis is to be found in the Sumerian *Dingir* ("Deity," here "Goddess") *Inanna,* later addressed by the Babylonians as Ishtar.[7] Presiding over the sacred marriage at the beginning of the New Year, she rode the Lioness of Time through the whole cycle of the year, finally regaining the next sacred marriage and resurrection of Tammuz. Inanna was worshiped from Anatolia to India from the fifth to the third millennium, with Mesopotamia providing the central temple nexus of her cult. The Thousand Names and their related doctrine surely connect back to this remote and far-flung area but survive fully only in their Sanskrit text.

II. FROM THE TARA PUJA CELEBRATING THE 21 TARAS

(Traditional Tibetan, adapted and edited from the text of Lama Chagdad Tulku, 1986, by C. Musès)[8]

To Troma (*Drolma*), the Green Tara

Namo arya Tara yeh. From the most perfect of places Troma is born from the green syllable TAM, its light shining forth to liberate beings who receive it.

Pupeh, Dupeh, Alokhé, Gandeh, Niwiteh, Shabda pra ti tsa SO HA AH HUNG! [21 syllables] i.e., Flowers, Incense, Light, Perfume, Food, Sound *pra ti tsa SO HA AH HUNG!* The form of Tara appears. In the center, in the heart, on a white moon appears a green TAM; thence many lights shine forth. All twenty-one Taras appear with this light. We invite the light of the unborn *dharmakāya*—the unobstructed Arya Tara's wisdom-essence. From Arya Tara's form, sweet nectars flow forth, entering through the crown, and our bodies become filled with ambrosia.

I salute you Troma, Divine Mother, Noble and Supreme One, throughout the ten directions and the three times. She who is the Saviouress, the swift one without fear, who gives with *TURÉ* whatever is needed. I bow to Her whose seed mantra is *SO HA*, Whose face is fashioned from a hundred full moons of autumn, Who gleams with the revealing light of a thousand stars—She who is the field through whom the six virtues are made manifest.

Salute Her who is the mound on the heads of the buddhas, Who fills the sevenfold worlds of Desire, Direction, and Space with the mantra *TUTTARÉ HUṀ*, Who controls them all; Whose fingers form the mudra of the Triple Gem to adorn Her heart, Whose wheel-emblazoned hand twirls about its own light and reaches to every direction, She who by Her laughter brings demons and the world under Her sway.

Salute Her who alone has the power to command the guardians of the foundation of our universe; Who sits surrounded by a radiant garland of flames, like the fire of a finished aeon, Who may turn the Wheel of the Law to our inclination, conqueror of great obstacles by Her tenfold mantra OM TARA TU TARÉ TURÉ SO HA.

Inside the great pot of jewels are the three syllables OṀ, AH, HUNG [rendered "Body, Speech, Mind"; cf. the fundamental Magian precept of love and truth in Thought (HUNG), Word (AH), and Deed (OṀ)]. May the two bodhicittas ripen naturally. Arya Tara's body becomes one with mine as Her rays are absorbed from now until enlightenment is reached, with mundane and supra-mundane happiness.

Salute the one Who holds the hare in the moon and the lake of the gods in Her hand, Who removes all poisons.

Salute Her whom all the assembly of gods serve and attend.

This is the Root or Primal Mantra of the Twenty-one Salutations. By recalling it at dusk or dawn it gives perfect protection from all fears, clearing impending consequences of one's past acts, so that one receives high empowerment, and everything in this life proceeds towards divine awareness. Hindrances will be negated; all that is wished for will be attained.

May we have the measureless strength to practice enlightenment in great waves, and may holy Tara ever protect us that we become unweakened and unerring.

III.

And in the following theophanies by JACQUELINE NORTHFIELD, Goddess and God take on humanity and find familiar resonances in our lives and in our visions and sacraments of love. As the poetess wrote to me, "These poems are written in the spirit of a tantric priestess seeking regeneration through her quest for the lost beloved, culminating in ecstatic union: not a crude androgyny of hermaphroditism, but a transformatively harmonious blossoming of both natures. Thus tremendous power is generated. By worshipping the presence-of-goddess in woman, the god-like presence in man is catalysed, and vice-versa." Then Goddess incarnates, and Isis rescues her Osiris.

The Goddess to a Young Bride

What has love to do with patience, gentleness, kindness
and all those virtues which adorn the shrinking bride
as bedazzled, bejewelled and besotted
she ascends to the bridal chamber?
No joking and no mockery could lighten this pregnant
    darkness
where all ornaments are stripped away
until we are dissolved and reborn
in light that seems a darkness to us
dreaming here below in our disjointed sleep

Temple Priestess Vision

O golden lion-hearted one
flowing through my veins like light
Defenceless I stand before you
my waters turning to wine
inflaming me with vision
of riding the skies on rapturous raptor wings . . .
O blood of my blood and flesh of my flesh
who can unlock the golden key of me—
I join with you again and again . . .
Knowing not if I drown or fly
I ask not to escape:
for if that light's too great to bear
I'd die to see thee standing there!

IV.

There is also a higher pregnancy, in store for all who will, as in
these lines (by KYRIL DEMYS).

Pregnancy

In nature's glass we feel
such primal flames
but by a scanted, dim reflection
from their powering source
that best we see and sense
in fitful heartbeats of our very flesh—

when mightily and with simplicity
love swells within
consuming us with joyous pregnancy
wherefrom we know
ourselves shall soon be born:
sunlit to live
in light that from our hearts
shall stream forever more.

V.

Two odes (by MUSAIOS).

To Maia

Spirit of light and of blessedness
Genius of Spring and of gladness
Goddess of love and fruition!
Thy form I see in May nights' scintillating skies
as scented breezes from Thy starry chariot blow
to fructify the barren earth of wintry days . . .

O teach my heart to sing the Silent Song
Instill into my soul its magic hue
Let tears of gladness mingle with the fragrant dew
of blooming gardens
ne'er again to part from joyous paeons
in the palace of the gods.

To Shakti

As dawn first burst against my opening eyes
I dreamed a last dream ere I woke to earth.
On golden air your fair form did arise
and fused my soul with light to give it birth.
One instant lived I as a new-blown breath
as fresh as that from soulless sylphs outbreathed,
in vernal fires my doubting died a death
that left my brow with wraiths of heaven wreathed . .
Then every atom, lustreless and dim
within me, drank your splendid smile and rose
upon the morn—a golden-chorused hymn

171

of perfumed pollen to the heavens rose.
Thus daily turns my dross to gold by Thee:
Thou and the dawn, divinest alchemy!

VI.

Some lines from the passionate rhapsody of France's great poet
PIERRE DE RONSARD, for whom Goddess incarnated in his sixties
as the lovely Hélène de Surgères (translation by C. Musès).

Je veus brusler pour m'en voler aux cieux
Tout l'imparfait de ceste escorce humaine . . .
en espérant quelques foys de taster
ton paradis, où mon plaisir se niche.

I long to burn, while mounting to skies,
All imperfection from this human rind . . .
Aspiring to taste and taste
Thy paradise, wherein my pleasure niches.

VII.

And from a vision of Goddess by LISA LYON:

I am your eternal bride
your wide, starry-eyed child
your daughter, your mistress
I am the fire in your loins
your mother, your lover
I stand here, pure sister
naked and vulnerable before you
I am the priestess, the star
one foot on earth and one on air
my perfumes are the heavy oils
of arcane art

in my flaming mandorla
I seek myself in all of you
your mouth, your eyes, your sex
they are mine
I want to fuse into a perfect child

172

a sacred child conceived in the wild
in Egypt
for each encounter with you is a wedding
an endless, ongoing ceremony

Editorial Note

Here is a lovely poem in high lyrical expression that we can all appreciate. But the same sentiments implemented literally would arouse the worst taboo of most cultures: the nightmare image of incest. This last contribution thus raises profound questions of the human yet transcendent vision of a total relationship with an ideal "Thou." Mystics of both sexes in the Christian, Indian, and Islamic traditions have experienced similar states of heightened perception and feeling. The Divine Beloved is felt as *all* social roles at once. This concept of a numinous and all-encompassing relationship enters deeply into the human transcultural psyche and throws profound light on our key point here: why such universal closeness lay at the basis of the incest taboo whose nature and origins fascinated both Freud and Jung, who never, however, fully sounded or resolved them.

Yet Freud, whose honesty is always endearing and admirable, wrote quite candidly in *Totem and Taboo* that "still in the end one is compelled to subscribe to Frazer's resigned statement, namely, that we do not know the origin of incest dread and do not even know how to guess at it." Indeed, both sociology and psychology have foundered on the reefs of incest. "Infantile regression" as an explanation, in the face of the mountains of anthropological fact, is patently not only inadequate but inappropriate to plumb the incest question.

The reason for these difficulties is that its psychological origin is veiled in the numinous, as an ontological fact and not merely a phenomenon of the human psyche. The "incest" is meant to be simply a role metaphor for a transcending, all-embracing, and apotheosizing relationship. In that transfiguring and hierogamic realm, the metaphor becomes sublime; but if one attempts to abuse it by literalness, then it can become sociological horror in many

173

cultures. It is here a matter of the highest regeneration or a mostly tragic degeneration, with little or no ground between except in the imputedly divine royal succession practice of certain ancient cultures (e.g., Egyptian, Iranian, Incan, and Polynesian) or in the social acceptance and cultural implementation and support of certain shamanic roles. For further discussion, see our contribution to the *Proceedings* of the Fourth Conference on Shamanism held in September 1987, edited by Ruth-Inge Heinze of the anthropology department of the University of California at Berkeley. *C.M.*

Notes

1. Cf. the Egyptian *Ma'at,* She-Who-Measures-and-Orders. *C.M.*
2. *Mantraśāstra Lalitā-sahasranāmam* with Bhāskararāya's commentary, translated by R. Ananthakrishna Sastry (Adyar, Madras, India: Theosophical Society Publishing House, 1976).
3. Instruments of magical evocation. *C.M.*
4. Thus forming the sacred 9, or ancient Egyptian ennead of divine powers, divided also into 5 + 4 domains of god- and goddess-regents in esoteric Taoism. *C.M.*
5. Her saving, eucharistic grace and power. *C.M.*
6. All the above references are from F. Hölscher, *Die Bedeutung Archäischer Tierkampfbilder* (Würzburg, 1972).
7. Adopted in the Hebrew "Esther" and the Phoenician Astarte, not to mention the great Germanic Goddess *Oster,* the origin of the later Christianized feast of "Easter." The Goddess still lives. *C.M.*
8. I am grateful to Janice Chase, moving spirit of the Santa Barbara Center of the Karma Thogsum Chöling, for drawing this beautiful prayer to my attention when we were discussing Tara and the rites of chöd after she had read the new introduction to *Esoteric Teachings of the Tibetan Tantra* (Musès 1982). *C. M.*

AVE ATQUE VALE

To rephrase Catullus' poignant "hail and farewell" we may well be saying it, in this critical era, to all past ages. What good we can salvage and promote for those who follow is the great question today.

From even a cursory study it soon becomes evident that the process of human history has been wasteful and destructive. This becomes even more evident when it is compared with the development of other systems of life forms on our richly endowed planet. The prime problem of our times, then, is how to optimize the development of human society, which means nothing less than global human society in an age of very fast feedback/feedforward loops generated by the electronic and electromagnetic communication technology that has pervaded the twentieth century and will continue, with advances in fiber optics and laser beams, to pervade the twenty-first unless some decisive historical discontinuity intervenes.

One of the first things history shows us is that it proceeds by overshoot and cutback, which is simply another form of the age-old learning process of trial and correction. Such correction is, of course, in terms of the best approach or approximation to some predetermined goal or selected standard by which results are valued and assessed.

So far so good. But what makes matters sticky in historical reality is that such predetermined standards have often been either not the most desirable in the long or even short term, or else were from the start riddled with unviable assumptions bound to bear bitter fruit. One of the commonest historical failings is for some current leadership to be so carried away by seductive features of its chosen aim as to become almost totally blind to the deleterious consequences of the wholesale adoption and application of such goals in practice. The usual historical process has been often disastrous in terms of unachieved social goals, especially since the advent of the new social caste of "scientists," who have come to speak with more social authority than any group since the ancient priesthoods.

As a few examples, we need but cite the host of synthetic drugs with harmful side-effects, the failure of centralized national economies that inhibit initiative and creativity, and the increasing failure of pollutive industrialization to achieve long term social good; not to mention the process of more efficient military technology resulting in long-term counterproductive feedback.

The Gulf War of 1991 is the latest case in point, which far outdid the bombings of Dresden and Nagasaki and engaged in the systematic and high-speed destruction of the life-support system of an entire nation's civilian population. It did not enter the military steersmen's tunnel vision that there is no cybernetic difference between a small-time terrorist setting off a bomb in a crowded cafe and his big-time counterpart dropping one on a crowded civilian air shelter. The essence of all such methods is their cybernetic idiocy: their utter lack of taking into account the counterproductive consequences they inevitably generate.

What, then, is the approach that will stop such short-term "success" methods with their built-in long-term failures from dominating human history more and more dangerously? The reason for the qualification "dangerous" is simple: current technology has so magnified the speed and magnitutde of consequence-loops, that the earth could actually be rendered unlivable if the processes that have dominated past human history are not now modified. And long before the planet became unlivable it would become plunged in such pervasive dissatisfaction that social unrest (and the resulting police-state lashbacks) would mount to exponential proportions.

The time scale for such critical phenomena is no longer comfortably long, and reliable projections place the crucial range of years between 1992 and 1999. It is then that the decisions will have been made and the steermanship done that will entrain the twenty-first century in a net of consequences, whether for good or ill.

Let us back up for a moment to the historical process of trial and correction, a more accurate term than "trial and error" since the latter if taken at face value could produce no improvement. The key factor here is to make reasonably sure that the values in whose service we do the correcting are viable in the long term; and, if not, to be flexible and aware enough to change them as soon as early warning signals arise, such as growing discontent. Short-sighted political leadership ignores this caveat with impunity.

We have paid lip-service to Copernicus but in reality have continued a most narrow anthropocentrism in our dealings with the natural environment. Carried away by obsession with the supreme importance of humans over anything else, we have well nigh forgotten how we necessarily depend on our own intestinal flora to keep alive and healthy, or how much we need one of the simplest life-forms—the diatoms of the phytoplankton—as an important factor of our oxygen supply, which is also ensured by the still not yet understood but tremendously pervasive and universal physical effect of gravitation without which all our atmosphere would dissipate into space in a trice. Thus gravitation is a biological necessity and ecology includes physics.

The choice is ours. Ask not for whom the bell tolls: it tolls for thee. Shakespeare adds to Donne some final words we disregard today at our peril: "We teach bloody instructions which return to plague the inventor, and even-handed justice condemns the ingredients of the poisoned chalice to our own lips." Let us take heed, and go forward towards health and sanity.

It is to point the way to such happier and viable alternatives that this book was written. Let us then step out into hope.

C. M.